made at home

a guide to simple sewing

by lisa stickley

Quadrille
PUBLISHING

this book is dedicated to aunty linda.
for her unwavering passion for life and
love, her support, and her wonderfully
colourful dresses.

editorial director jane o'shea
creative director helen lewis
project editor lisa pendreigh
designer claire peters
photographer ben anders
stylist katie sellers
illustrator lisa stickley
production director vincent smith
production controller ruth deary

first published in 2010 by
quadrille publishing ltd.
alhambra house
27–31 charing cross road
london wc2h 0ls
www.quadrille.co.uk

british library cataloguing-in-publication data
a catalogue record for this book is available from the
british library.

isbn: 978 184400 237 5

printed in china.

it probably started with lego, but for as long as i can remember, i have always been making, creating, painting and drawing – everything from fairy cakes with fluffy butter icing to hand-cut paper flowers and wooden picture frames (using all of dad's offcuts from the shed). in our house *the reader's digest family book of things to make and do* from the 1970s was well used.

for a while my mother used to make some of her own clothes and mine, but it was my aunty daphne that i spent most of my sewing and knitting time with at an early age. on saturdays, mum, aunty daph and i made regular morning shopping trips, returning armed with cream cakes to spend the afternoon making things.

i learnt a lot from both my mum and aunty. in my early teens i was given a hand-turning sewing machine and then, just before starting my university degree, i acquired an electric one. while i trained professionally as a printed textile designer, i have never specifically had any formal training in dressmaking or pattern cutting. i just have a great passion for creating and with a lot of practice have learnt that, with some simple techniques and an ability to stitch two layers of fabric together, you can create some rather lovely and often very useful items.

similar to cooking, it is important to start with good 'ingredients'. handsome items can be made using the simplest of techniques, but will look absolutely stunning if the fabric you start with is good quality. this doesn't mean you need to spend a fortune on lavishly expensive fabrics, you just need to keep an eagle eye out for the diamonds in the rough and search out pieces you love and those suitable for the project in hand.

the idea of this book is to share my passion for homemaking; if you have even just an ounce of desire to be creative, i hope that *made at home* will give you the inspiration and confidence to make some items for yourself. we are not talking couture – intricately detailed and fabulously expensive finished products – but lovely handmade items for you and your own home. things that will brighten and smarten up your rooms, add an original, personal touch and be used and loved for all their (perhaps slightly imperfect) perfection.

when writing the instructions for this book (which did result in more than a few very late nights with quill and desk lamp!) i have tried my best to be as clear and straightforward as i can. .there are a mix of projects throughout, ranging from easy to slightly more challenging. as with most things it is much easier when you know how, so i would encourage you stick the radio on, have a cup of tea at the ready and have a go. as they say, practice makes perfect and the main thing is to enjoy the process!

happy sewing,

lisa.

basics

fabrics and basic equipment.

i have suggested specific
weights and types of fabric
for each project. below are
descriptions of some familiar
fabrics to help you choose what
to use. different fabrics produce
different end results; all i would
say is that if the ingredients are
good, the item you are making
will be all the better for it.

fabrics

plain weave the most basic form of textile weave
– also referred to as taffeta, canvas or duck – is
most readily available in cotton, silk, and wool
(amongst others). a hardwearing fabric; the
heavier weights are great for upholstery and the
medium weights for soft furnishings.

denim a heavy weight fabric, often indigo dyed,
most obviously used for jeans. constructed in a
diagonal weave, it is extremely hardwearing. ideal
for pouffes and door stops.

twill like denim, twill has a characteristic diagonal
weave. available in cotton, wool and silk in light
and medium weights, examples are chino, drill,
tweed and serge. a great fabric for many projects
in this book. in a beautiful medium weight cotton,
linen or silk, twill is perfect for cushions and blinds.

canvas a heavy weight fabric that, like denim,
is extremely strong. in a beautiful linen this can
be rather stunning and is perfect for heavier duty
projects where sturdiness is required.

satin or sateen, woven in either cotton or silk.
with a glossy, luxurious finish, satin is more
commonly used for garments. i used it for the
pin tucked cushion (see pages 110–13) where it
gave a wonderful finish. but unless you are well
practiced, i recommend cotton satin rather than
silk, as it can be tricky to handle.

taffeta a plain woven fabric, most commonly in
silk, of which there are two distinct types: piece-
dyed taffeta and yarn-dyed taffeta. the former is
much softer and more suitable for linings with the
latter being much stiffer. often used for wedding
dresses, this deluxe fabric lends itself beautifully
to curtains and cushions.

calico an unbleached plain cotton weave
available in light, medium and heavy weights.
sometimes it is not fully processed but also
available as pre shrunk. used in the fashion
industry for 'toiles' (mock-up garments), calico
is great to practice with as it is cheap. it also
serves well as a sturdy lining.

herringbone weave a distinctive 'v' shaped
pattern most commonly produced in wool for
suiting, this cloth is also hard wearing and a good
option for many interior projects.

damask available in endless patterns, the
designs are woven into the cloth rather than
printed. available in silk, wool, linen, cotton or
synthetics, a wonderful fabric for home projects.

brocade very similar in process to the damask
above the brocade has raised pattern woven
into the fabric to give the appearance of an
embroidered finish. classic luxury at its best.

dupion silk a silk with a subtle textured crisp
finish and a glorious sheen. wonderful for
cushions and lighter weight curtains.

tasar silk this softer silk is a good medium to
heavy weight fabric; perfect for a number of
home projects. i used this for the winter curtain
(see pages 80–5) and it gave a great finish.

equipment
the main items you will need are illustrated
opposite, but there are always other useful bits
and pieces that can be added to your tool box as
and when you need them:
A3 paper, A2 paper, old newspaper
tailor's chalk
curved needles (light and upholstery weight)
masking tape
quick unpick
thread snips
cotton bias binding (12mm and 20mm wide)
polyester wadding

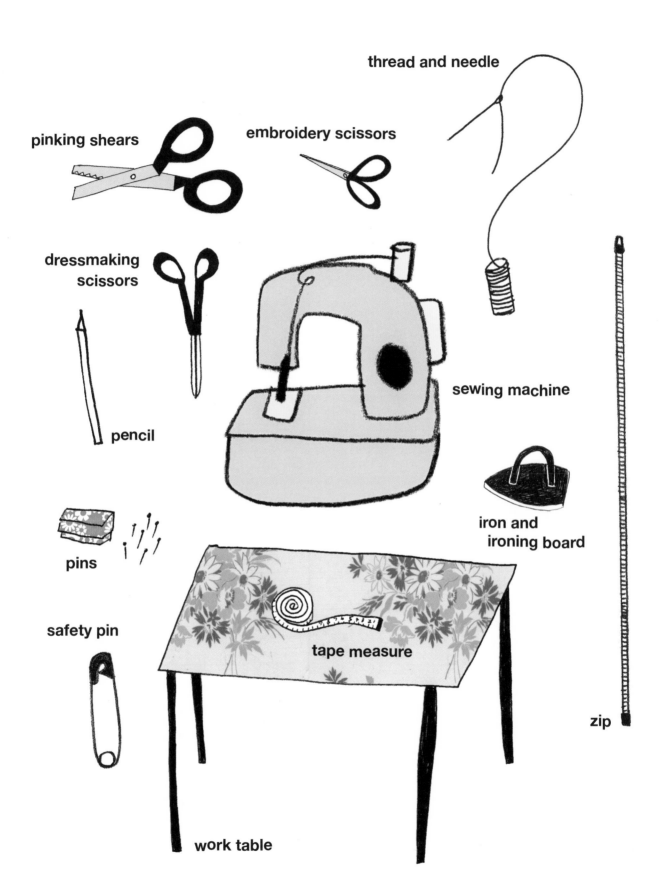

thread and needle

pinking shears

embroidery scissors

dressmaking
scissors

pencil

sewing machine

iron and
ironing board

pins

safety pin

tape measure

zip

work table

stitches.

although not all of these stitches have been mentioned throughout the projects in the book, they are important basics skills needed when sewing, and are great to know. you can dip in and out of this chapter as you work through the projects and perfect your skills with the nuts and bolts of sewing.

small backstitch

when hand sewing you need to fasten the thread at the beginning and end of the stitching with a small backstitch. this is much neater than simply knotting the thread. sew a small initial stitch making sure not to pull the thread right through the fabric, then sewn over two or three times more to fasten the thread in place.

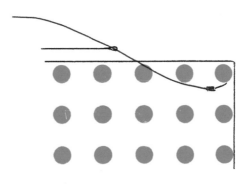

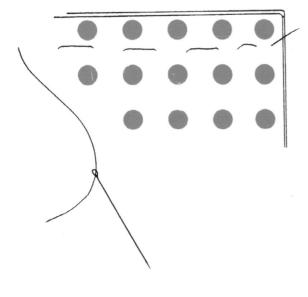

tacking

tacking is a temporary stitch, which is longer than normal, with the stitches usually around 1–2cm in length. it is used in many sewing projects and can be an alternative to pinning. the thread from the tacking stitch is removed once the fabrics have been machine stitched together (it's helpful to use a contrast colour thread for easy removal). this stitch is particularly helpful for larger projects such as winter curtains or bed spreads. to stitch two or three pieces of fabric together take your needle and a short length of thread (50cm should do) and begin at one end with a small backstitch. stitching from right to left, push the needle right the way through the fabric and back towards you in one movement. repeat this along the edge of the fabric with roughly 1cm long stitches, about 3mm from the final seam line. pull the stitches reasonably taught but not too tight as they will need to be removed once the seam has been machine stitched. fasten at the end with a small backstitch.

slipstitch

slipstitch is regularly used for hemming and sewing the side seams in curtains, and other projects where the aim is to achieve an almost invisible stitch on the front side of the fabric. it is very helpful indeed to have a suitably sharp needle for this. with the prepared hem turned, pressed and ready, and holding the fabric with the wrong side facing and the seam at the top, begin with a secure backstitch in the turned hem. sewing from right to left and keeping the stitches as evenly spaced as you can, push the needle through the turned hem and carefully pick up two or three strands of the facing fabric on its wrong side. the idea is that the thread is only visible as a small point on the front side of the fabric. having brought the needle back through to the wrong side run it along the hem for 5mm then repeat the stitch. repeat this along the length of the hem and secure with a small backstitch to finish.

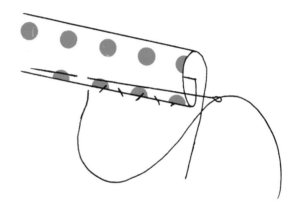

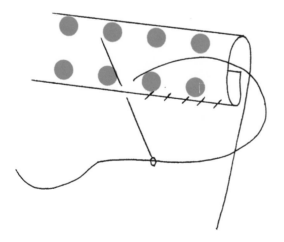

hemstitch

hemstitch is very similar in purpose to the slipstitch and has the same aim to achieve an almost invisible stitch on the front side of the fabric. with the same method of picking up only two or three threads from the wrong side of the front fabric, work small diagonal stitches along the hem making them as neat and even as possible, and fasten the thread at the start and finish with a small backstitch.

gathering stitch

gathering stitch is designed to do exactly what the name suggests: gather up fabric, when an article requires it, for example a curve on a valance or fitting a shoulder on a sleeve. for extra strength two parallel rows can be made about 3mm apart, either on the right or wrong side of the fabric. start with a backstitch to fasten the thread, then run the needle in and out several times before pulling the needle through, making each stitch around 3mm long. continue this along the length of the fabric. repeat for the parallel row if necessary, making sure that stitches in the second row line up with the equivalent stitches in the first row. pull up the threads together and wind around a pin to hold in place.

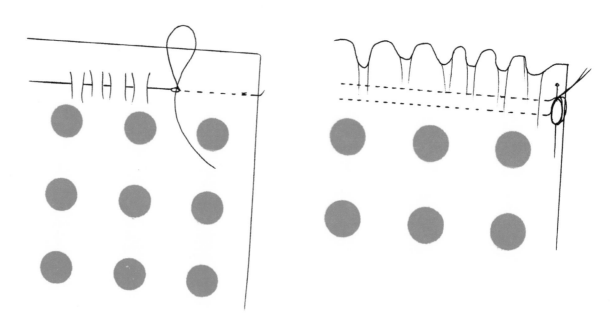

backstitch

this is the hand-sewn equivalent to machine stitching and is very strong, so generally used when fitting zips by hand or stitching when there are too many layers of fabric to go through the machine. start with a small backstitch to fasten the thread and make the first stitch from front to back around 5mm finishing with the needle to the front in one movement, pull up the thread. go back 2.5mm to fill in the gap then repeat with the next 5mm long stitch. continue this as far as required; the aim is to make a continuous line of thread on both sides of the fabric.

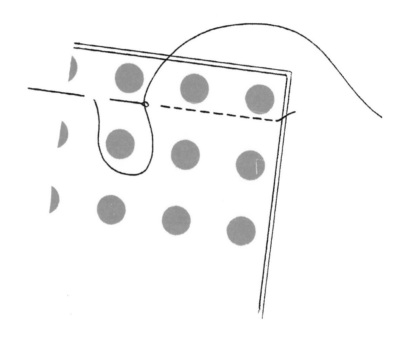

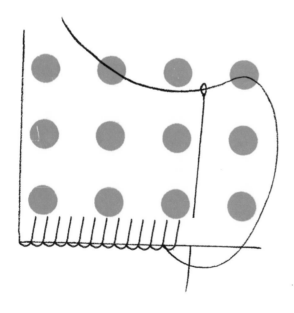

blanket stitch

this stitch is designed to join two pieces of fabric together whilst creating a decorative stitch along the edge of the fabric at the same time. starting with a small backstitch to secure, take the needle through the fabric from front to back around 6mm from the fabric edge. hold the thread under the point of the needle and pull the needle through forming a loop. pull the thread just taught (but not too tight) up to the edge of the fabric and continue keeping the stitch as even as possible to give a nice finish. fasten with a small backstitch at the end.

seams.

a couple of essential seaming
methods to get you started.

flat seam

this seam is used to join two pieces
of fabric together using a single line
of stitching, far enough from the raw
edges to prevent the fabric fraying.
generally a seam of 10mm to 15mm is
recommended. with the two pieces right
sides together either, pin or tack along
the line you are going to stitch and then
machine the seam securing with a back
stitch at the start and finish. on the wrong
side open out the seam and press flat to
give a neat finish. if you need to secure
the seam (known as a topstitched seam)
then press both allowances to one side
and stitch through all layers of the seam
allowance from the right side, 3mm from
the first seam.

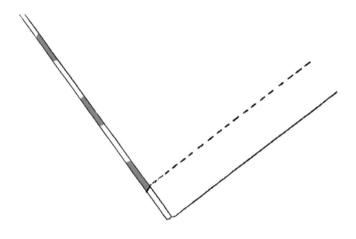

french seam

this seam is generally used for finer fabrics with a tendency to fray, for example net or unlined curtains. also it is a seam commonly used when making shirts, blouses and other more delicate garments. its purpose is to trap the raw edge of the fabric within itself and is therefore not suitable for more heavy weight fabrics. with the wrong sides of the fabrics together pin and stitch a 6mm seam. trim any frayed edges and press the seam fully out with the right sides facing. pin and stitch a second seam this time 12mm wide enclosing the raw edges as you sew.

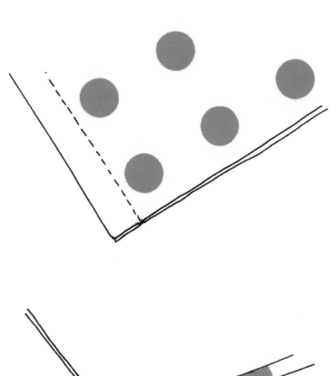

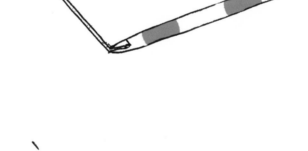

corners and curves.

useful tips to help you tackle corners
and curves with neatness and ease.

turned corners

when stitching a corner
and before turning out
to the right side, trim the
seam allowance diagonally
across the corner to
achieve a neat finish: a
good technique to use
when making square
cushions, placemats and
laundry bags.

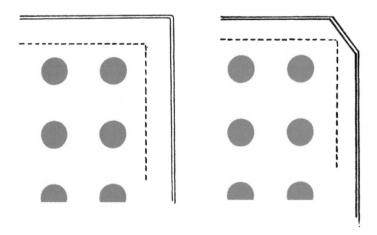

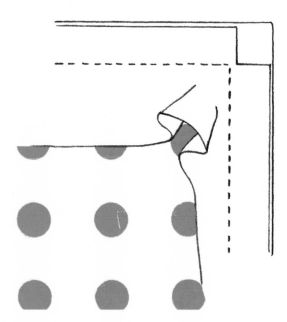

boxed corners

a useful technique to use when making
the outdoor cushion or similar. just
before you reach the corner point cut into
the seam allowance at right angles to the
seam. complete stitching up to this point
and reinforce the corner with a few back
stitches across the diagonal. continue to
stitch the seam down the other edge and
repeat on the following corners.

clipping corners and curves

clipping simply means making small regular cuts in the raw seam allowance to help achieve neater corners or curves. clips reduce the bulk of the fabric when corners are turned through, and allow the fabric to lie flat when a stitched curve would otherwise pull it out of shape.

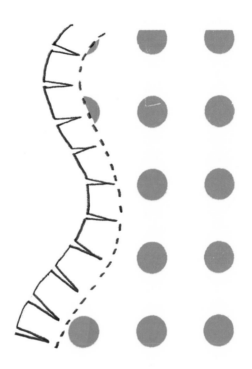

finishes.

some basic techniques and
additional attractive finishes
useful for any number of projects.

bias binding
fold the bias binding lengthwise and pin
in place over the raw edge of the fabric.
stitch as close to the turned edge of the
binding as possible, taking care to catch
the underside of the binding as you sew.
tuck the raw edge of the binding under for
a neat finish at each end, and backstitch
the start and finish to secure the seam.

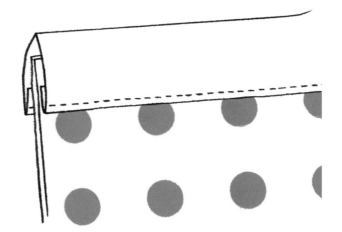

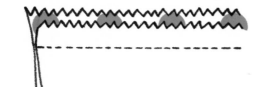

pinking
this is a technique to
prevent a seam from
fraying simply by cutting
along the raw edge of the
seam with pinking shears.

piping

various types of ready made piping are available from good haberdashers, but you can prepare your own using binding and cord. simply wrap the binding around the cord and stitch down the length of the binding as close to the cord as possible with the raw edges lined up. to stitch piping into a cushion attach it to one side of the cushion first, using a zip foot on your machine helps you sew close to the cord. if you are working on a square cushion it is a good idea to make the corners slightly rounded, which helps the piping sit flat against the fabric. for a neat finish trim the cords of the piping (leaving the casing intact) so they butt up against each other. tuck the raw edges of the casing under themselves to achieve a neat finish. to finish the cushion tack the second side of the cushion in place and machine all three layers together all the way around (make sure to keep the zip half open so you can turn the cushion out to the right side when finished! an easy thing to forget… i have done this many a time!)

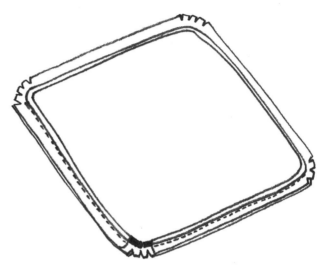

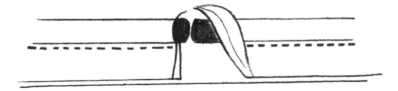

fitting a zip.

a simple method of fitting a zip. it may look a touch daunting but practice on some odds and ends. you will see it's easy once you know how.

a neat way to finish the end of a zip is to add a zip end. this is simply a small piece of fabric, 3cm x 4cm, which will cover the raw end of the zip. place the small zip end piece and the cut end of the zip right sides together. machine in place with a 1cm hem. fold the unstitched side of the zip end back 1cm, then fold the whole piece around to the back side of the zip being careful to keep the raw edge tucked underneath. machine in place sewing a little to the right of the first seam just sewn, making sure to catch the tucked side of the zip end in as you stitch.

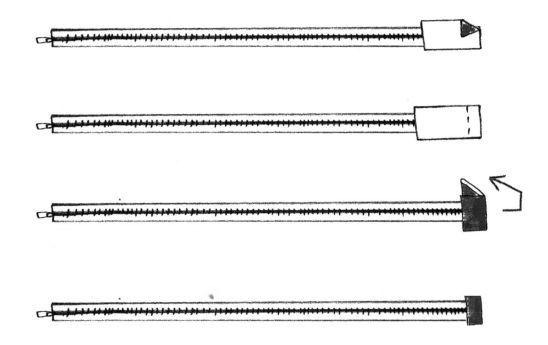

prepare the two pieces of fabric the zip is to be fitted to by folding and pressing a 1cm hem along the edge of each panel. change over to the zip foot on your machine. starting with one panel, line the pressed edge of the panel up with the open end of the zip. i find this easier to machine without pinning in place and with the zip open by only a couple of centimetres. depending on the type of zip foot you have on your machine, it is often easiest to stitch the panel to the zip with the fabric on the left of the zip, then turn the zip around to attach the second panel. a little practice is always handy, so if you have a spare zip lying around then this is a great time to have a go with a scrap of fabric to get your confidence up! machine the zip in place making sure to back stitch at the start and finish to secure the seam. repeat this on the opposite side of the zip, this time machining the other panel in place. make sure to line the panels up with each other, and the open end of the zip.

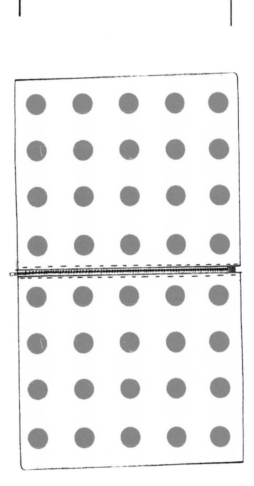

buttonholes.

an extremely useful technique to master. the trick is to be patient when stitching by hand. also do not pull the thread too tight – regular, taught, neat stitches are what you are after.

to create a buttonhole by hand
you will need to cut a slit in the fabric in the position required; the slit needs to be the width of the button you are using. you will then need a strong thread to secure your buttonhole with buttonhole stitch, ideally matching the colour of the thread to the fabric you are working on. buttonhole stitch is similar to blanket stitch but sewn so the stitches butt up against each other. fasten the thread to start and then take the needle through the fabric from back to front, again around 6mm from the fabric edge (although this may vary depending on the thickness of the fabric). before you pull the thread taught, loop it around the point of the needle. the aim is to form a knot on the raw edge of the fabric. continue this all the way round the buttonhole until you have created a secure, sealed, neatly stitched hole.

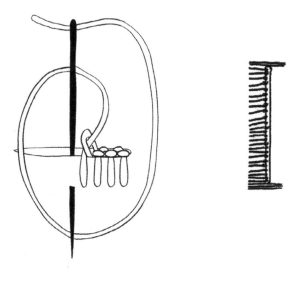

to create a buttonhole with your sewing machine you will require a special buttonhole foot. if your sewing machine has this then it should also come with simple instructions to follow. as these instructions vary from machine to machine, it is tricky for me to explain the buttonhole technique in detail. the general principle, however, is the same in terms of the size of buttonhole to be made; the only exception is that you machine stitch around the buttonhole before cutting the slit.

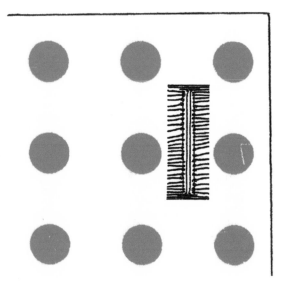

quilting.

quilting is one of the oldest household crafts; it is a method of holding two layers of fabric together with a third layer of wadding in between for extra warmth.

it is a technique that has been practised for hundreds of years and, alongside patchwork, is celebrated all over the world with museums and galleries displaying examples of this highly skilled and varied craft. many ladies (and I am sure gentlemen too) indulge in the process, creating stunning and sometimes intricate works that can only be produced with passion and patience.

simpler quilting techniques, such as that described on pages 114–17, can be used to create lovely items. if the fabrics used are well selected and elegantly luxurious, with a relatively easy process and a little time and effort you can make a quilt to be proud of. if you find the bulk of the fabric too great to fit under the arm of your sewing machine, the three layers of fabric and wadding can be stitched together by hand, but for a small bedspread with a simple grid pattern and some crafty use of fabric rolling, the quilting technique should be achievable on the machine. once the fabric is tacked in place, work from the outer edge to stitch the first rows of the grid, rolling the fabric as you go until you reach the centre. repeat on the opposite side to complete, meeting in the centre. turn the bedspread by 90 degrees and repeat the process until the whole grid is finished.

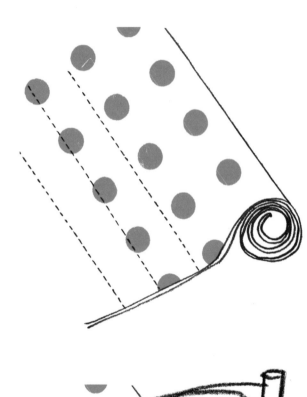

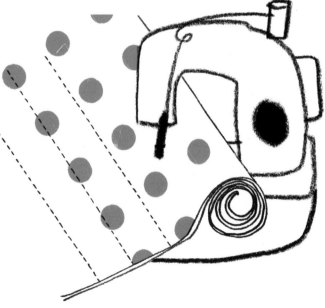

for the **kitchen**

napkins.

things you need

per napkin: 1 piece of medium weight cotton or linen fabric, approximately 50cm x 50cm for a regular size napkin.

this is a guide. the same method will easily work for a rectangular napkin (for example, 60cm x 40cm) or for dinky afternoon tea napkin (for example, 30cm x 30cm) and pretty much any other size within this arena!

napkins can be made in a variety of sizes and from many different types of cotton or linen. to me they are essential to every meal and i feel lost without one. they are very easy to make and can be coordinated to style your table for a tremendously terrific tea! i like to mix and match, so for a relaxed supper i regularly use an eclectic collection of vintage plates with mismatched linens. for a smarter, more formal sunday roast i might use something similar to the napkins shown here.

hem the napkin.

fold a 1cm hem over to the wrong side along each edge of the fabric piece and press. repeat this all the way around for a second time so the raw edge of the fabric is concealed, take care not to pull the fabric out of shape and to make neat corners as you press. pin in place then stitch all the way around, sewing as close to the inside edge of the turned hem as possible. backstitch at the start and finish to fasten the seam.

stitch the buttonhole.

for an extra posh napkin it is a nice touch to add a buttonhole to one corner. i saw this done on a british airways napkin from the 1960s; it is a great idea, especially when wearing a white shirt and eating spaghetti! the buttonhole needs to be of a sufficient size to fit over a shirt button (approximately 15mm). the napkin can then be secured neatly to the top button of a shirt, offering maximum protection from bolognaise splashes. see page 24 for how to add a buttonhole.

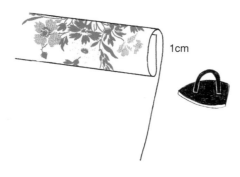

1cm

placemats.

things you need

per placemat: 2 pieces of medium weight cotton, approximately 43cm x 34cm.

from an intimate dinner for two to a family filled sunday lunch for twelve, it is a favourite task of mine to lay the table. alongside napkins, side plates, water and wine glasses, knives, forks, spoons, salt and pepper pots, vintage candle holders and pretty flowers, placemats are an essential part of every table setting. they mark your guests' territory at the table and provide a great starting point to plonk all the other bits around and about them. they are also rather good at protecting your table!

stitch the seams.

place the front and back panels together with right sides facing. pin around three sides. on the fourth side pin 6cm in from each end, leaving a nice gap through which to turn the placemat right side out when stitched. with a 1cm seam allowance stitch where you have pinned. backstitch at the start and finish to fasten the seam. clip the corners (see page 19), then turn the placemat out to the right side.

close the opening.

press the seams neatly where you have stitched. to finish the open side turn the raw edges under and press so they are level with the stitched edge. stitch the opening, stitching as close to the edge as possible for a neat finish. backstitch at the start and finish to fasten the seam.

bon appetit!

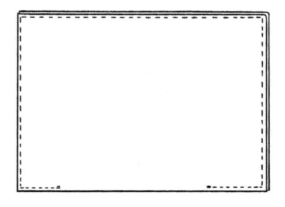

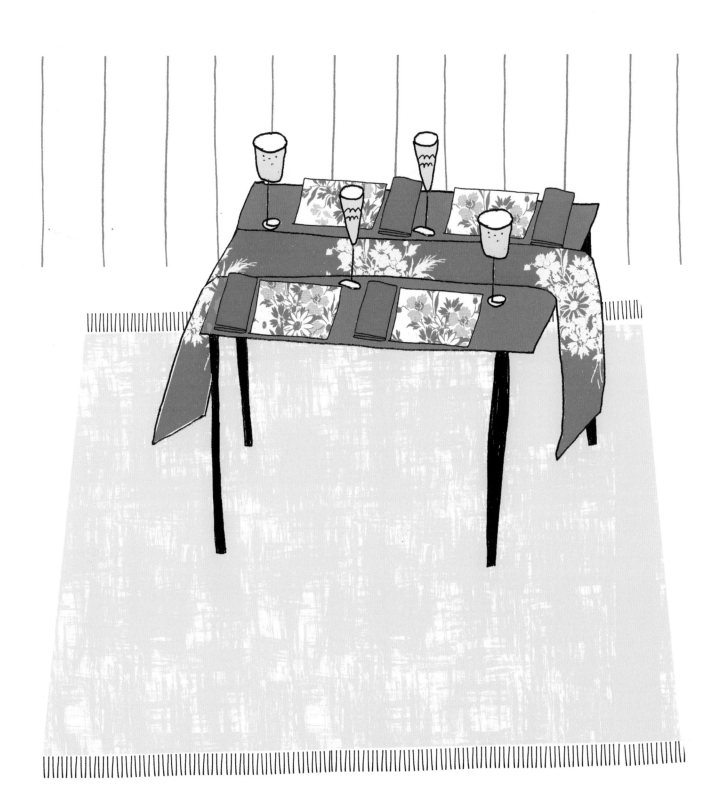

table runner.

things you need

1 piece of medium weight cotton or linen, approximately 34cm by the length of your table plus 84cm.

the table runner is a neat addition to the dressed table, omitting the need for a full tablecloth. combined with placemats, napkins, eclectic china and glassware, a runner lends an air of sophistication to the modern table. the finished size of the runner obviously depends on the size of your table, but a guide for an average sized dining table is a width of 30cm or thereabout, with an overhang either end of 40cm or so.

hem the table runner.

fold a 1cm hem over to the wrong side along each edge of the fabric piece and press. repeat this all the way around for a second time so the raw edge of the fabric is concealed. pin in place. stitch all the way around stitching as close to the inside edge of the turned hem as possible for a neat finish. backstitch at the start and finish to fasten the seam.

tea cosy.

things you need

1 sheet of paper or newspaper, A3 or larger.

2 semi-circular pieces of medium weight cotton for main body (i have used a damask).

2 semi-circular pieces of light weight cotton for lining.

1 rectangular piece of cotton for loop, 4cm x 10cm or thereabouts.

2 semi-circular pieces of 4oz polyester wadding for insulation.

tea, cake and a little herbie hancock on the radio in the background are all particular favourites of mine. this is a nice easy project to ensure that your tea will be steamy hot even after the cake is gone!

cut out the pieces.

to make sure the cosy fits, lay your teapot on its side on to a large piece of paper. draw a semi-circle around the teapot adding an extra 5cm on all sides to make the pattern for the main body and lining. to cut out an even shape fold the semi-circle down the centre lengthwise and use the best drawn line as the cutting guide. using this pattern, cut out the fabric for the main body and lining. cut the wadding 4cm smaller than the template all the way round.

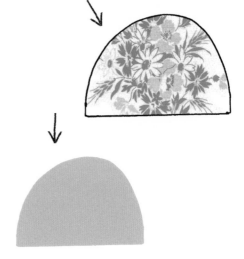

make the loop.

fold a 1cm hem over to the wrong side along each long edge of the fabric piece and press. then fold the fabric down the middle lengthwise so the two turned edges meet. press and pin. stitch along the open side, stitching as close to the edge as possible for a neat finish. backstitch at the start and finish to fasten the seam. stitch the same line along the opposite side to finish the loop.

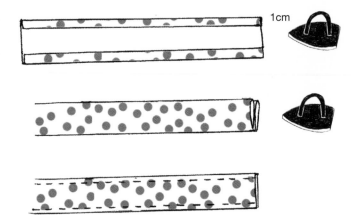

make the main body.

place the two main body pieces right sides together. fold the prepared loop in half and sandwich it between the two main body pieces at the centre top, with the raw edges of the loop in line with the raw edges of the main body. pin in place. pin the two body pieces together along the curved edge. stitch together with a 5mm seam allowance catching the loop into the seam as you sew. fold a 1cm hem over to the wrong side around the base and press, but don't stitch this just yet. turn the tea cosy right side out.

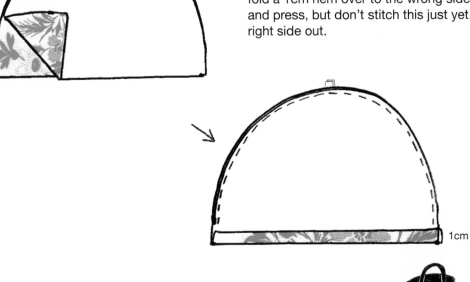

make the lining.

place the two lining pieces right sides together. pin in place along the curved edge. stitch together with a 5mm seam allowance. press. fold a 2cm hem over to the wrong side around the base and press, but don't stitch this just yet.

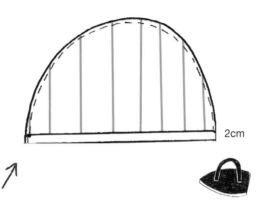

2cm

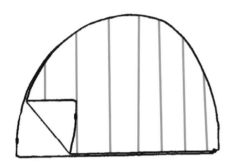

finish the tea cosy.

with wrong sides together slot the lining inside the main body. on each side sandwich a cut piece of wadding in between the main body and lining and flatten into place. pin the base of the main body to the lining making sure the pressed hem is neatly lined up and any stray bits of wadding are tucked in. stitch the base together all the way around, stitching as close to the edge of the hem as possible for a neat finish.

put the kettle on for a cup of tea, and I recommend a generous slice of angel cake!

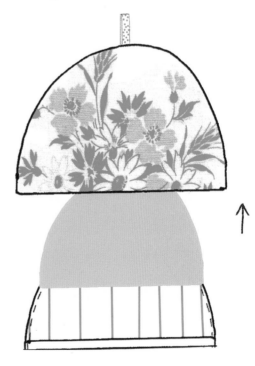

egg cosy.

things you need

1 sheet of graph paper with a 5cm square grid (or hand draw a grid in pencil onto plain paper if you can't find any graph paper).

1 piece of medium weight cotton or light weight linen for main body, 30cm x 30cm will be plenty.

1 piece of medium weight cotton for lining, 30cm x 30cm will be plenty.

1 rectangular piece of cotton for loop, 4cm x 8cm or thereabouts.

2 semi-circular pieces of 4oz polyester wadding for insulation, 30cm x 30cm will be plenty.

radio four on the wireless (well, dab these days), a selection of newspapers and two dippy eggs with buttered soldiers are the ingredients for my perfect sunday morning. here is a lovely way to keep your eggs cosy while you make the coffee.

cut out the pieces.

using the template on page 138, cut out a paper pattern for the main body and lining. using this pattern, cut out the fabric for the main body and lining. cut the wadding 4cm smaller than the template all the way round.

make the loop.

fold a 1cm hem over to the wrong side along each long side of the fabric piece and press. then fold the fabric down the middle lengthwise so the two turned edges meet. press and pin. stitch along the open side, stitching as close to the edge as possible for a neat finish. backstitch at the start and finish to fasten the seam. stitch the same line along the opposite side to finish the loop.

make the main body.

place the two main body pieces right sides together. fold the prepared loop in half and sandwich it between the two layers at the centre top, with the raw edges of the loop in line with the raw edges of the main body. pin in place. pin the two body pieces together along the curved edge. stitch together with a 5mm seam allowance catching the loop into the seam as you sew. backstitch at the start and finish to fasten the ends of the seams. turn out to the right side and press. fold a 1cm hem over to the wrong side around the base and press.

make the lining.

place the two lining pieces right sides together. pin in place around the curved edge. stitch together with a 5mm seam allowance. backstitch at the start and finish to fasten the ends of the seams. press. fold a 1cm hem over to the wrong side around the base and press.

finish the egg cosy.

on each side sandwich a wadding piece in between the main body and lining and flatten into place. pin the base of the main body to the lining making sure the pressed hem is neatly lined up and any stray bits of wadding are tucked in. stitch the base together all the way around, stitching as close to the edge of the hem as possible. backstitch at the start and finish to fasten the seam. this bit can be a little fiddly on such a tiny item, but with a little patience and practice you will have egg cosies galore.

put the toaster on to prepare the soldiers!

apron.

things you need

heavy weight cotton canvas cut to size (see template on page 139).

4m length of bias binding in a contrasting colour (2.5cm wide).

2 pieces of webbing for side ties, each 120cm long.

2 pieces of webbing for neck ties, each 65cm long.

protect your blouse in the most stylish fashion while baking, kneading, whisking, roasting or any other foodie related tasks in the kitchen. with ties at both the neck and sides, this is a one-size-fits-all apron and is easy to make too.

add the bias binding.

starting on one straight side pin the bias binding all the way around the main apron piece. to start each length of binding turn the raw edge under by 1cm. as you reach the corners cut the binding with a 1cm excess and tuck this under to conceal the raw edge and give a neat finish. stitch this in place all the way around taking care to catch the bias binding on both sides as you sew. backstitch at the start and finish to fasten the seam.

make the ties.

at each end fold a 1cm hem over twice. stitch a line to secure the ends and prevent fraying. on the wrong side position each tie at either the neck edges or top of each straight side, 5cm in from the edge of the main apron piece. pin in place. stitch the ties; for extra strength stitch a rectangle and then add a cross in the middle.

bake a cake to test the apron, ideally a victoria sponge!

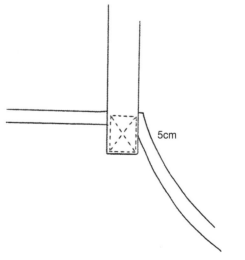

5cm

pinny.

things you need

1 piece of light weight cotton or linen, approximately 54cm x 62cm.

1 piece of contrast cotton fabric for the tie, approximately 8cm x 150cm.

to protect your lower half when performing lighter kitchen duties or to simply assist when lots of hand wiping is called for, this neat little pinny is the perfect addition to any kitchen.

hem the pinny.

fold a 1cm hem over to the wrong side along the bottom edge and both sides of the fabric piece and press. repeat this for a second time so the raw edge of the fabric is concealed. pin in place. stitch the three sides stitching as close to the inside edge of the turned hem as possible for a neat finish. backstitch at the start and finish to fasten the seam. fold the fabric piece in half to find the centre and mark this point with a pin at the top raw edge.

make the tie.

fold a 1cm hem over to the wrong side
along each edge and press. then fold
the fabric down the middle lengthwise so
the two turned edges meet and press to
make a crease. taking care to keep the
pressed crease sharp, unfold the tie. next
find the centre point of the tie and mark
with a pin. position the main body piece
and the tie together, matching up the
central pins. place the main body piece
just below the pressed crease of the tie.

1cm

make the pleats.

at the marked centre of the main body
piece make a small 1cm pleat. then
make another 1cm pleat either side
of this first pleat, leaving a 6cm gap
between each pleat. press and pin the
pleats in place as you go, making sure
the pin heads are aiming downwards
so they are still visible once the top half
of the tie is folded down. fold the top
half of the tie down to cover the pleated
top edge of the main body. pin in place
along the entire length of the tie.

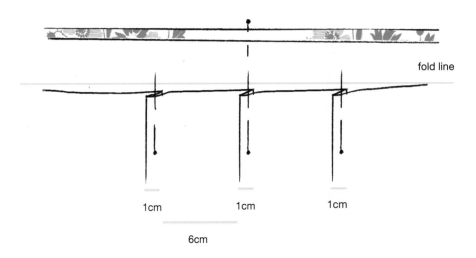

fold line

1cm   1cm   1cm

6cm

sew it all together.

starting at one end of the tie, stitch all
the way along pinned edge, taking care
to enclose the pleated main body as you
sew. backstitch at the start and finish to
fasten the stitch.

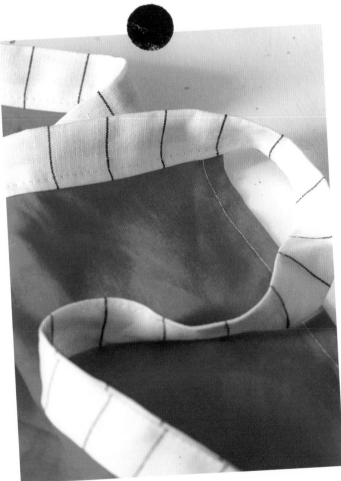

let the housewifey chores
begin... alternatively, don
a pair of fluffy mules to
accessorise your pinny
and kick back with a well-
deserved g&t!

shopping bag.

things you need

1 piece of medium or heavy
weight cotton canvas,
approximately 54cm x 96cm.

2 pieces of medium or heavy
weight cotton canvas for
the handles, approximately
60cm x 12cm.

apples, pears, milk, eggs and iced
buns always look lovelier in a chic
floral or stripy cotton shopping bag.
this shopper is easy peasy to make
and is a wonderful way to recycle
old curtains – not to mention helping
the cause by cutting down on the
plastic carrier. super strong for lots of
shopping, this bag is neat enough to
fold up and pop in your handbag.

make the handles.
for each handle fold a 1cm hem over to
the wrong side along all four edges of
the fabric piece and press. then fold the
fabric down the middle lengthwise so the
turned edges meet. press and pin. stitch
together all the way around, stitching as
close to the edge as possible for a neat
finish. backstitch at the start and finish to
fasten the seam.

make the bag.

fold the main body in half widthways with right sides facing, so the two side edges meet. pin in place. stitch both sides and the bottom seam together with a 1cm seam allowance. trim the three seam edges with pinking shears.

hem the bag.

fold a 1cm hem over to the wrong side along the top edge of the bag and press (it helps to use the end of the ironing board to do this). repeat this for a second time so the raw edge of the fabric is concealed. pin in place then stitch all the way around the top edge stitching as close to the inside edge of the turned hem as possible. backstitch at the start and finish to fasten the seam.

make the bag gusset.

flatten out the bag so that the two side edges are lined up in the centre. open out the bottom edge into square. mark a triangle at the top and bottom corners of this square as follows. from the point of the triangle measure 6cm in along each edge and mark with tailor's chalk. draw a line across to join these two marked points together. stitch across the chalk line. backstitch at the start and finish to fasten the seam. it is a good idea to stitch these seams twice for double strength. trim the excess corner fabric with pinking shears. repeat for the second corner. this makes a 10cm wide gusset. turn the bag right side out.

6cm

attach the handles.

on the right side of the bag position one end of a handle 10cm in from the side seam and 6cm in from the top edge. position the other end of the handle to match at the opposite side. pin in place. stitch the handle to the bag; for extra strength stitch a rectangle and then add a cross in the middle. repeat on the other side of the bag with the second handle.

fold up and place in your handbag ready for any impromptu shopping trips!

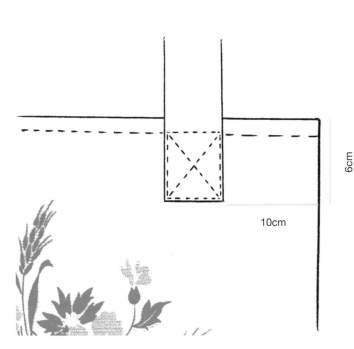

6cm

10cm

for the **living room**

café curtain.

things you need

1 piece of light weight cotton fabric for curtain panel, at least 2cm larger all round than the size of your window.

light weight cotton fabric for the loops, 4cm x 12cm per loop (you will need one loop for every 10cm of curtain width).

wooden dowel.

emulsion paint and paintbrush (a tester pot should do the trick).

2 screw hooks and screw eyes.

inspired by the classic café curtain, this simple and rather attractive window treatment is ideal for covering the lower half of any window (although preferably one with a wooden frame). it affords privacy without blocking out all the light, and is a great way to add colour and pattern to a room at the same time.

measure up.
to determine the size of the curtain panel required, measure your window and add 4cm to both the height and the width to give a 2cm seam allowance on each side. cut the panel piece to size.

make the loops.
fold a 1cm hem over to the wrong side along all four sides of each fabric piece and press. then fold the fabric down the middle lengthwise so the two turned edges meet. press and pin. stitch all the way round the loop, stitching as close to the edge as possible for a neat finish. backstitch at the start and finish to fasten the seam. repeat this for all loops.

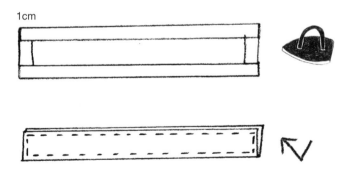

1cm

hem the curtain panel.

fold a 1cm hem over to the wrong side along each edge of the fabric piece and press. repeat this all the way around for a second time so the raw edge of the fabric is concealed, take care not to pull the fabric out of shape and to make neat corners as you press. pin in place then stitch all the way around stitching as close to the inside edge of the turned hem as possible. backstitch at the start and finish to fasten the seam.

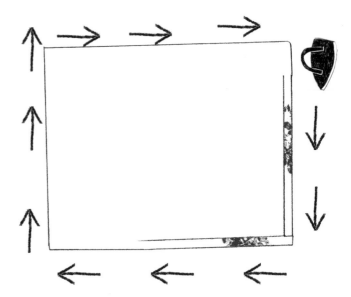

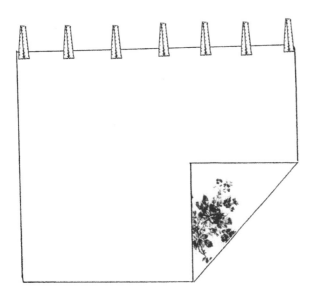

attach the loops.

fold each of the loops in half widthways and press. starting at the outer edges of the curtain panel and working in towards the centre, position the loops on the wrong side of the panel at the top edge at regular intervals of 10cm (or thereabouts). to make attaching the loops easier, lay the two ends of each loop side by side rather than one end on top of the other (this makes the curtain less bulky and easier to stitch). pin each loop in place. stitch the loops to the curtain panel stitching 5mm in from the top edge. backstitch each loop a couple of times to fasten securely. press.

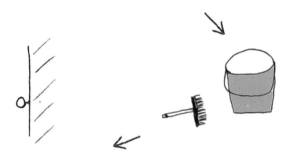

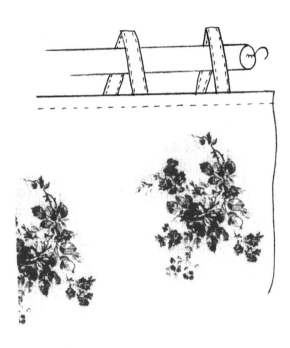

hang the curtain.

cut the wooden dowel to the width of the window frame allowing a small gap for the hooks and eyes (1cm at either end should do the trick). paint the dowel the colour of your choice – i used a regular white emulsion. once the paint is dry, screw the hooks into either end of the dowel and fix the screw eyes in place on the window frame. pass the dowel through all the loops, then hook the complete curtain and dowel in place on the hooks. there you have it!

seat cushion.

things you need

1 sheet of paper or newspaper, A3 or larger.

medium weight cotton or linen for the main cushion (around 50cm x 100cm per cushion should do it).

2 pieces of medium weight cotton for the ties, 4cm x 40cm.

foam or wadding for the filling (50cm x 50cm x 4cm thick should be plenty, but check against your seat pattern template to be sure you have enough).

1 upholstery zip (to match the width of the back of your chair seat – see fitting a zip on page 23).

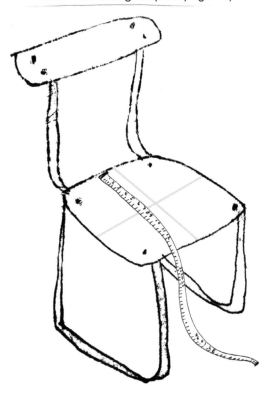

wooden kitchen chairs – available in a wondrous collection of shapes and sizes – are rather lovely in my eyes, but after a lengthy sunday lunch or a five-course dinner they can become a touch uncomfortable for the derrière area. to maximise comfort, add a nice soft cushion. seat cushions are relatively easy to make and with ties at the back to fix them in place, they are the perfect accompaniment to a long-lasting lunch.

measure up.

measure the depth and width of the chair seat in question; a seat is often wider at the front than the back and this needs to be taken into account when drawing out the pattern template. for the seat pieces draw the exact shape of the chair seat on to the paper and then add a 1cm seam allowance all the way around. you will also need pattern templates for the side panels, front panel and back panel. the side panels are the same length as the sides of the seat pieces, and 6cm deep. similarly the front panel is the same width as the front of the seat piece, 6cm deep, and the back panel is as wide as the back of the seat piece, and 6cm deep.

cut out the pieces.

cut your fabric pieces using the pattern templates. you will need two main seat pieces, two side panels, one front panel and one back panel.

make the ties.

fold a 1cm hem over to the wrong side along all four sides of each fabric piece and press. then fold the fabric down the middle lengthwise so the two turned edges meet. press and pin. stitch all the way round the tie, stitching as close to the edge as possible for a neat finish. backstitch at the start and finish to fasten the seam. repeat this for all ties.

fit the zip.

fit the zip to the back panel as follows: cut the panel in half lengthwise and fold a 1cm hem over to the wrong side along the length of one side on each piece. press and pin. then follow the instructions for fitting a zip as given on pages 22–3.

make the gusset.

close the zip fitted in the back panel. with right sides facing pin the ends of the two side panels to each end of the back panel so the raw edges meet. stitch together leaving a 1cm seam allowance. backstitch at the start and finish to fasten the seam. press the seams open. repeat this to join the front panel to the other ends of the side panels, pressing the seams open once sewn. you should end up with a floppy rectangle shape, which is the cushion gusset.

join the seat pieces.

with the right sides together pin the gusset to the bottom seat piece. i find it easier to start with the back and work my way round, pinning as i go and making sure the seams meet as planned in the corners. follow the instructions for sewing box corners as given on page 18. stitch the gusset in place with one continuous seam, leaving a 1cm seam allowance. backstitch at the start and finish to fasten the seam. (make sure the zip is open for the next bit as you will need to get a hand in to turn the cushion cover right side out once you have finished stitching.) repeat this process to join the gusset to the top seat piece. turn the cover right side out and press the seams (the edge of the ironing board helps with this).

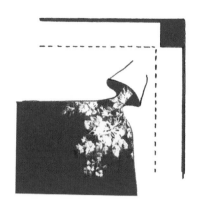

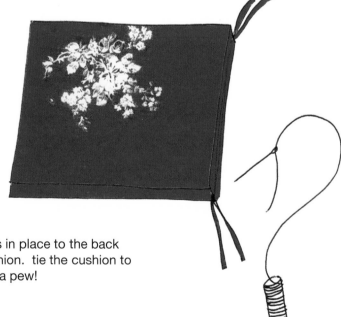

add the foam.

using the seat pattern template, cut the foam or wadding to the correct size to fit your cushion cover. you will need to use a sharp stanley knife and take extra care when cutting. stuff the cushion cover with the cut foam.

add the ties.

hand stitch the ties in place to the back corners of the cushion. tie the cushion to the chair and take a pew!

roman blind.

things you need

1 piece of main fabric, (the size of the window to be covered plus 5cm in width and plus 15cm in length for the header and hem).

1 piece of lining fabric, (the size of the window to be covered plus 5cm in width and plus 15cm in length for the header and hem).

bias binding, 25mm wide, 2cm longer than the width of the blind.

1 wooden dowel, 9mm in diameter, the width of the blind less 2cm.

binding tape (calculated by the number of rows and the height of the blind: you need one vertical row every 30cm across the width of the blind).

metal rings (calculated by the number of rows and the height of the blind: on each row you need a ring every 15cm across the width of the blind).

1 wooden header board (sanded and smoothed) the width of the window by 2.5cm and 5cm.

large screw eyes (quantity to match number of rows of tape).

strong cord (double the height of each row plus the distance from the top of each row across to the side of the blind).

1 cleat for the window

upholstery tacks and hammer

brackets and screws to fit the header board above the frame

wooden beads (optional)

fantastically neat and relatively easy to make (with a bit of patience), the roman blind is my first port of call when a window needs dressing. a medium weight cotton drill or indian duppion silk works well for this blind.

measure up.
to determine the size of the blind panel required, measure your window and add 5cm to the width and 15cm to the height. cut the main piece and lining fabric to size, making sure to cut as straight as possible.

seam the main panel.
place the main panel and lining pieces together with right sides facing. pin around three sides leaving the top open. with a 1cm seam allowance, stitch where you have pinned. backstitch at the start and finish to fasten the seam. clip the corners (see page 19), then turn the main panel out to the right side. push the seam and corners out fully, pressing as you go.

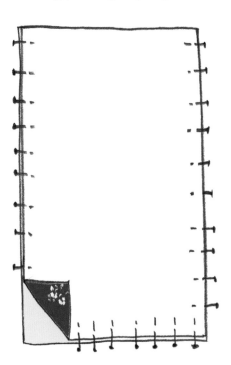

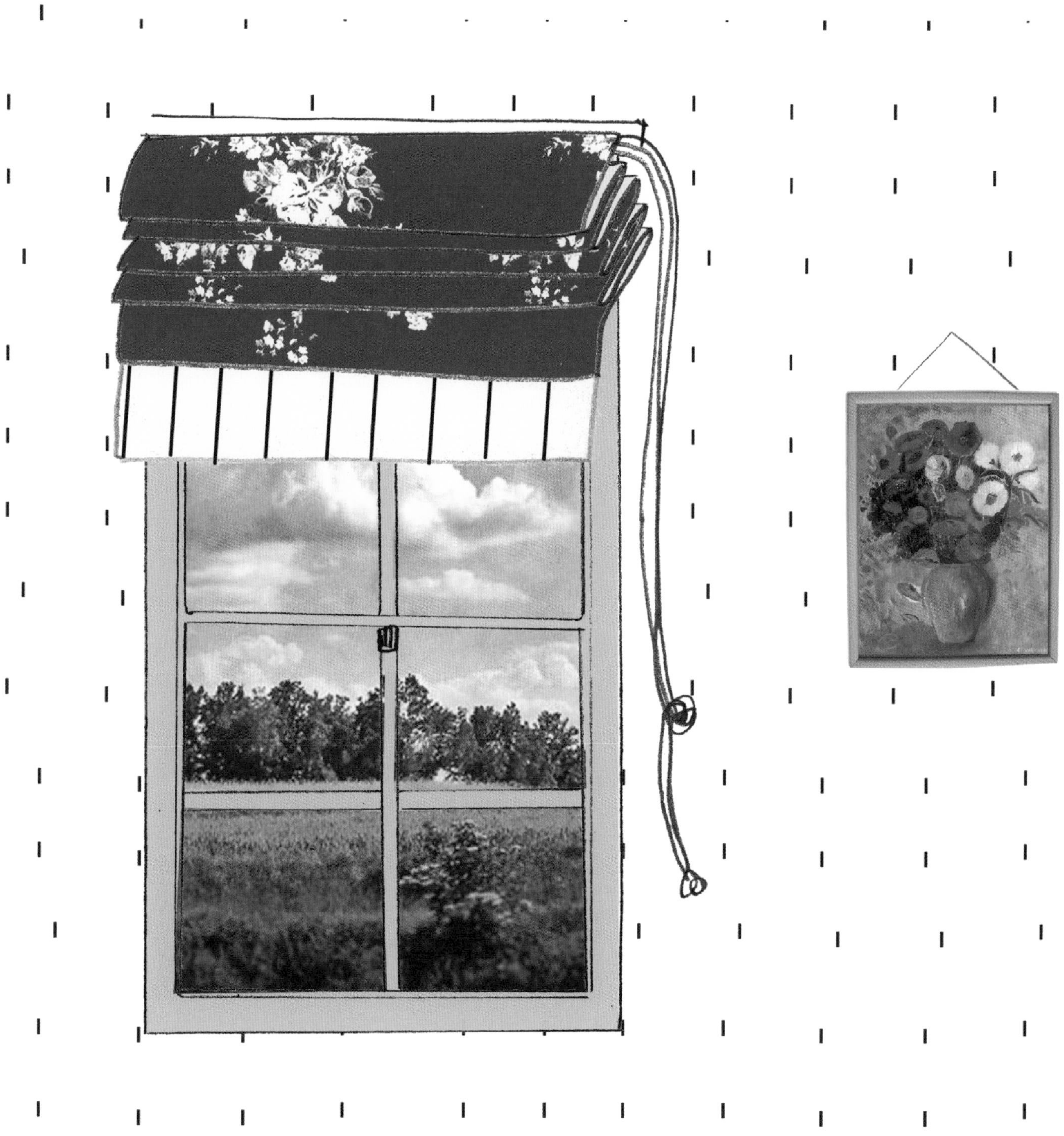

bind the main panel.

pin the bias binding along the top edge of the main panel. turn the raw edge of the binding under by 1cm to give a neat finish. stitch this in place all the way along taking care to catch the bias binding on both sides as you sew. backstitch at the start and finish to fasten the seam.

mark up the dowel casing.

lay the blind out flat with the lining face up. using a metre rule or straight edge and tailor's chalk or soft pencil, measure 14cm from the bottom and draw a horizontal line across the blind. draw a second line just above the first to mark the casing for the dowel. the casing must fit the dowel rod snugly rather than be too loose: 12mm should be fine to fit a 9mm diameter dowel rod but this may vary slightly depending on the weight of the fabric.

add the tape.

position the strips of tape vertically on the blind, working from the upper casing line to the top edge. starting at the outer edges of the panel and working in towards the centre, position the strips of tape 1cm in from the outer edges and then at equal intervals of 30cm (or thereabouts). when you are happy with the position of each strip, mark these lines on to the blind with the straight edge and tailor's chalk. pin or tack each of the strips in place tucking the ends under to conceal the raw edges as you go. stitch each strip in place. start each line of stitching from the top so the fabric does not pucker. backstitch at the start and finish to fasten the seam. slipstitch by hand the ends of each strip of tape to neaten.

stitch the dowel casing.

stitch the two horizontal casing lines. backstitch at the start and finish to fasten the seams.

attach the rings.

position the metal rings along each strip of tape, 15cm apart, making sure that the rings form exactly level horizontal lines across the blind. securely hand stitch the rings in place.

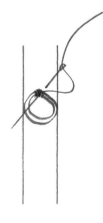

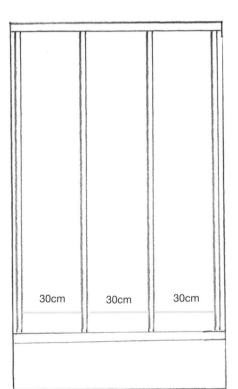

30cm   30cm   30cm

add the dowel.

unpick the side seam along
one edge of the dowel casing
to make an opening. slot the
dowel in place. slipstitch by
hand to re-seal the opening.

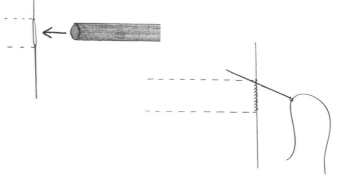

attach the blind to the header board.

position the top 15mm of the blind, lining side
down, over the edge of the header board.
hammer tacks all the way across the top edge
to fix in place.

add the screw eyes.

fix the screw eyes to the underside of the
header board directly level with the rows of
metal rings on back of the blind.

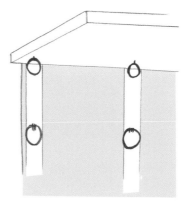

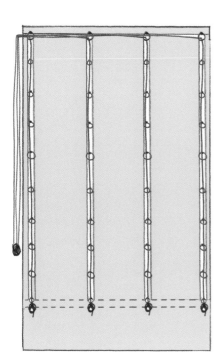

add the cord.

cut a length of cord for each individual row of metal rings on
the blind: each cord must be double the height of the blind
plus the distance from the row of rings to the side – so each
cord will vary in length as the distance to the side varies.
thread each cord through its row of rings and across all the
screw eyes. knot each cord to the bottom ring of its row.
knot the cords together just beyond the last screw eye and
again at their ends to keep them tidy. trim the cords to the
same length and attach the wooden beads (not essential
but a nice touch).

hang the blind.

fix the brackets and the header board above the window
frame. at a comfortable height attach the cleat to the side
of the window frame (or the wall if this is easier) for securing
the cord when the blind is pulled up. to set the pleats in the
blind, keep in the pulled-up position for the first few days.

bolster.

things you need

1 piece of medium weight cotton or linen, 64cm x 49cm (when hand stitching the zip)

or

2 pieces of medium weight cotton or linen, each 33cm x 46cm (when machine stitching the zip)

2 discs of cotton or linen, 21cm in diameter

2 buttons (mismatched vintage ones are good for this)

1 upholstery zip, 46cm long

1 feather-filled bolster, 46cm long by 20cm in diameter

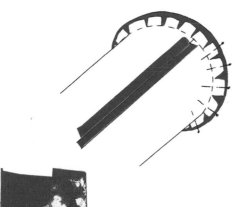

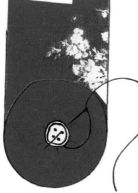

traditionally used on the bed, the bolster is great for plumping up when reading and snuggling up to when sleeping. as well as providing extra support, for me, they are equally fabulous for dressing up a sofa, armchair, daybed or chaise longue!

add the zip.
when using a sewing machine, fitting a zip is much easier with two panels of fabric. i used two panels of contrasting fabric for the bolster pictured opposite. to fit the zip between two panels of fabric, fold a 1cm hem over to the wrong side along the length of one side on each piece. press and pin. then follow the instructions for fitting a zip as given on pages 22–3. if you choose to use a single panel of fabric the technique is the same, however i recommend fitting the zip by hand as keeping the excess fabric out of the way of the sewing machine needle is particularly tricky.

join the main panels.
if using two panels you will need to join them together. with right sides facing, place the long edges of the panels together so the raw edges meet. pin and stitch with a 1cm seam allowance. backstitch at the start and finish to fasten the seam. press the seams open.

fit the end panels.
prepare the main piece for fitting the end panels by making a round of 1cm cuts, 2cm apart, at each end. with the zip half open, pin the end discs in place. stitch with a 1.5cm seam allowance. this is a little tricky so take your time: if you need to add a little pleat here and there to make it fit, then do.

attach the buttons.
turn the cushion cover right side out. with tailor's chalk, mark the centre point at each end. hand stitch the buttons in place, gathering the fabric in slightly to create a puckered effect. finish with a double knot and wind the excess thread around the button.

add the bolster.
stuff the cover with the feather bolster and zip up.

patched cushion.

things you need

4 pieces of light weight linen or medium weight cotton damask or linen in the following sizes:

1 large front panel, 52cm x 28cm.

1 medium front panel, 52cm x 16cm.

1 small front panel, 52cm x 12cm.

1 back panel, 52cm x 52cm.

1 upholstery zip, 50cm long.

1 piece of cotton fabric for zip end, 1cm x 3cm.

1 feather-filled cushion pad, 50cm x 50cm.

cushions are a fantastic yet simple way to update any room large enough to house a chair or sofa. they can be easily made in a variety of shapes, sizes and fabric combinations.

if you are using patterned or vintage fabric, keep to a particular colour scheme for an elegant eclectic look. or, for a bolder look, really mix things up with complimentary colours, patterns and shapes for a bright and modern statement.

in this instance i have teamed my favourite linen of the moment – a deep petrol blue with a floral print – with a plain oatmeal linen and a panel of vintage cotton damask.

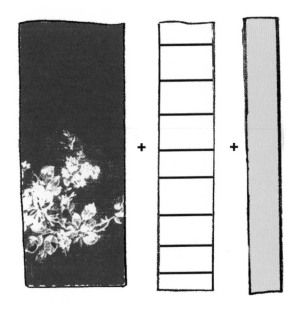

join the panels.

with right sides facing, pin the small and medium panels together along one long edge and stitch with a 1cm seam allowance. backstitch at the start and finish to fasten the seam. place the large panel and unstitched side of the medium panel together, with right sides facing. pin and stitch with a 1cm seam allowance. press the two seams open.

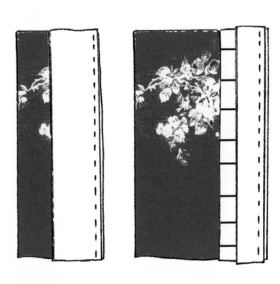

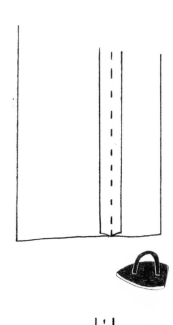

hem the panels.

fold a 1cm hem over to the wrong side along the bottom edge of the front panel and press. repeat this for the back panel.

add the zip

attach the zip end to the zip as given on page 22. unzip the zip to over half way. (this is so you will be able to get a hand in to turn the cover right side out once you have finished stitching. i have forgotten to do this on many occasions; it is very annoying as you have to unpick and start this bit again!) follow the instructions for fitting a zip as given on pages 22–3, placing the two panels right sides together making sure they are lined up with the zip edge. If the top of the cushion is slightly out do not worry, the essential bit is that the zip edge is lined up. use the zip edge as your straight line to work from to make a neatly stitched square. pin the panels in place. starting from the 'zip end' corner, stitch the three edges of the cushion cover together. trim the raw edges of the seams with pinking shears to neaten.

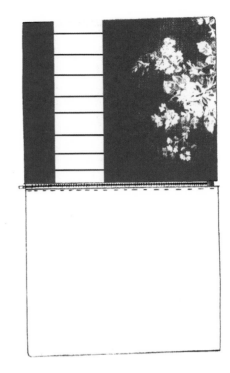

add the cushion pad.

turn the cushion cover right side out and press. stuff with the feather pad, et voilà!

antimacassar.

things you need

1 piece of light weight cotton,
36cm x 42cm (or thereabouts).

2 buttons (optional).

during victorian and
edwardian times it was
very fashionable for the
chaps to groom their hair
with a concoction of palm
and coconut oils. named
macassar oil. this pomade
was not overly popular with
the housewives of the time
as it had a tendency to soil
the permanent fabric on
the head of the armchair
or sofa. to overcome this
problem, these inventive
ladies covered the backs
and arms of their seats with
a fabric cloth that could
be removed periodically to
be cleaned... and so the
antimacassar was born.

the addition of a couple of buttons,
hand stitched to the back of the
chair, is an excellent way to hold
the antimacassar in place.

hem the panel.

fold a 1cm hem over to the wrong side along each edge
of the fabric piece and press. repeat this all the way
around for a second time so the raw edge of the fabric is
concealed, take care not to pull the fabric out of shape
and to make neat corners as you press. pin in place then
stitch all the way around stitching as close to the inside
edge of the turned hem as possible. backstitch at the
start and finish to fasten the seam.

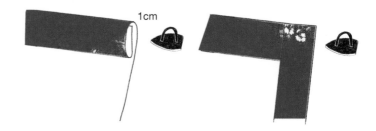

1cm

stitch the buttonholes.

add two buttonholes to the top edge of the antimacassar,
one in each corner. to hold the antimacassar in place,
hand stitch the buttons to the back of the armchair so
that they match up with the buttonholes.

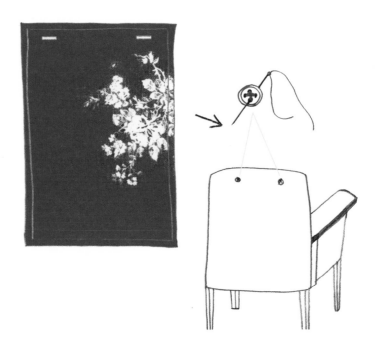

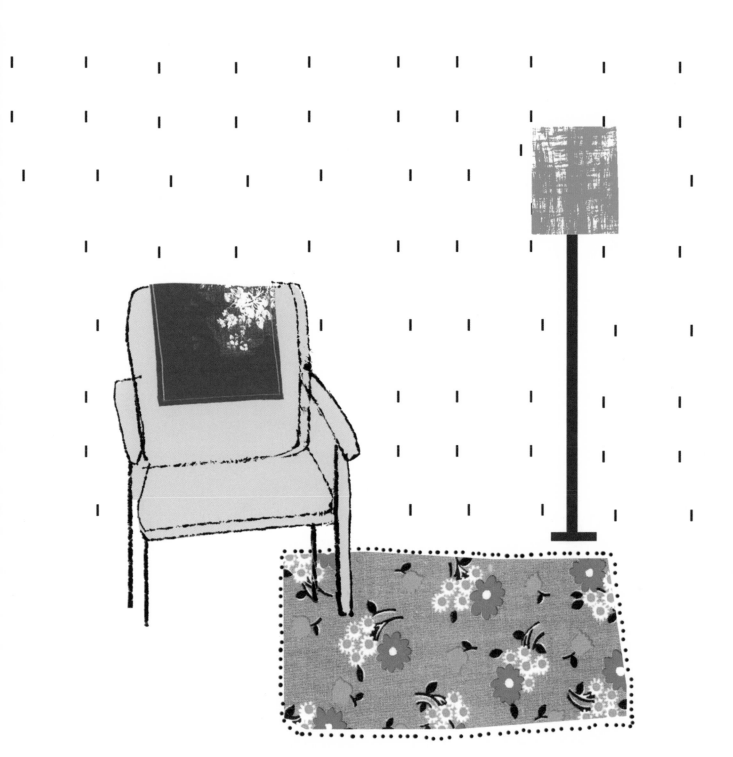

draft excluder.

things you need

2 pieces of light or medium weight petrol blue linen, the first measuring 42cm x 42cm and the second measuring 26cm x 24cm.

1 piece of light or medium weight oatmeal linen, 56cm x 42cm.

1 piece of medium weight cotton for the mouth, approximately 24cm x 24cm.

2 buttons.

a little scrap of linen for his fork shaped tongue.

stuffing (i have used old scraps of fabric as stuffing; as well as being a great bit of recycling, it makes the snake nice and weighty so sebastian stays put).

if, like me, you suffer from drafty doors then sebastian the draft excluder is the chap for you! he doubles up as a guard snake at the same time, so watch out for ankle nipping when you walk past. this is a really easy project to make; the beauty of this design is that it only takes a little tweak here and there – a change of colour, a longer tongue, a different eye position – to create a whole new personality of snake.

join the panels.

with right sides facing, pin the short edge of the oatmeal panel and the larger blue panel together and stitch with a 1cm seam allowance. backstitch at the start and finish to fasten the seam. place the remaining blue panel and unstitched side of the oatmeal panel together, with right sides facing. pin and stitch with a 1cm seam allowance. press the two seams open.

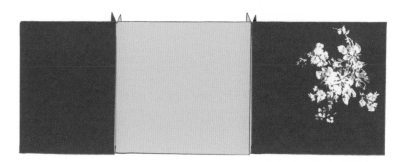

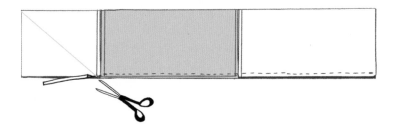

make the body.

with right sides facing, fold the fabric in half lengthways. pin and stitch the long edges, starting at the end of the larger blue panel but stitching only up to the end of the oatmeal panel, leaving the smaller blue panel unstitched. backstitch at the start and finish to fasten the seam.

make the tail.

lay the body out flat with the long seamed edge closest to you. using a straight edge and tailor's chalk draw a line across the smaller blue panel from the bottom right corner (at the seam line where it joins the oatmeal panel) to the top left hand corner. cut through both layers of fabric 1cm below this line, removing the bottom triangle shape you have just marked out. this will form the tail.

make the head.

lay the body out flat again, this time with the long seam running down the centre of the body. on the larger blue panel (head end) mark a point on the top edge, 12cm in from the corner. mark another point 12cm in from the bottom corner. draw two lines to join these points to the centre of the side edge, at the end of the seam. cut through both layers of fabric, 1cm outside these lines, removing the two outer triangle shapes you have just marked out. this will form the head.

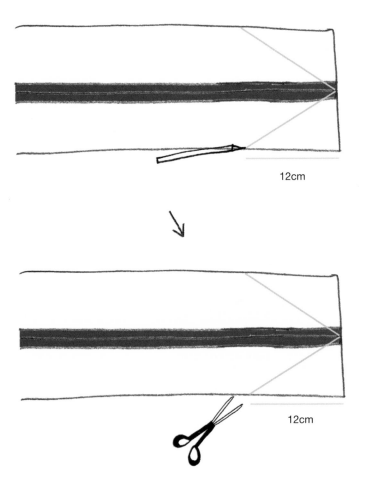

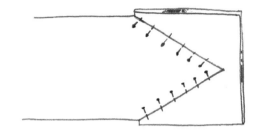

make the mouth.

with the right side facing inwards, fold the fabric piece for the mouth in half. slot this folded panel into the point you have just cut on the head piece; the folded edge must butt right up to the two corner points of the main head piece. working along one side at a time, pin the top layer of the pointed head piece to the top layer of the mouth panel. turn over and repeat on the other side. now stitch all the way around the mouth, following the line of the point, with a 1cm seam allowance. backstitch at the start and finish to fasten the stitch. this can be a touch fiddly but if you lay the mouth panel flat so the point is open as far as it can go, it just takes a little time and patience. start at the point on the one side and work your way around, taking care at the corners of the mouth. if a little pleat is required here and there, that's fine. it will simply add to the snake's personality. trim any excess fabric from the mouth panel with pinking shears (any waste can be used for stuffing).

stuff the snake.

turn the snake right side out, making sure all corners and crevices are fully turned out. your work should now resemble a floppy snake-like character. stuff the snake, starting at the mouth and working down to the tail. when you get to the pointed tail end, have a needle and thread at the ready. continue to stuff and stitch as you go, tucking the raw edges under and using blanket stitch (see page 15) to close the seam.

add the finishing touches.

once your snake is fully stuffed and the tail end stitched up, you are ready to add its eyes and tongue to bring him to life! i securely stitched two buttons on the top of sebastian's head as a pair of eyes. then i cut a fork-shaped snake's tongue from a scrap of the oatmeal linen, which i hand stitched to the middle of his mouth.

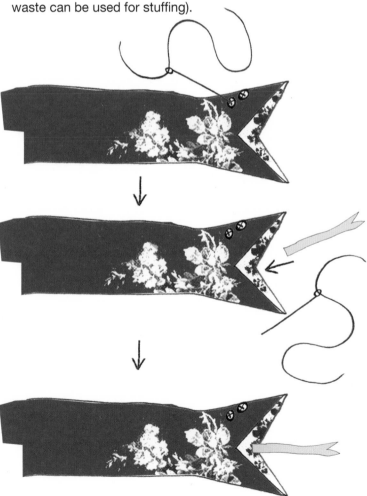

pouffe.

things you need

for the lining:

1 piece of heavy weight calico, 43cm x 147cm.

3 discs of heavy weight calico, 46cm in diameter.

42cm length of sew-in velcro, 2cm wide.

for the outer body:

1 piece of cotton drill, denim or similar weight fabric, 43cm x 147cm.

3 discs of cotton drill, denim or similar weight fabric, 46cm in diameter.

150cm length of piping.

double-ended upholstery needle.

4 buttons.

stuffing (either scraps of fabric or wood shavings).

there is nothing more relaxing than sitting in a comfortable armchair with your feet up on a pouffe, which also works very well as emergency seating if your lounge is overflowing with guests. when making them at home, stuffing with scraps of fabric creates a firm and weighty pouffe whilst putting all those waste bits and pieces to good use. alternatively wood shavings work equally well.

make the lining.

take two of the calico discs and measure 28cm across the diameter. mark a straight line across the circle at this point and cut along the line. repeat for the second disc. fold a 1cm hem over to the wrong side along the straight edges of the part circle and press. repeat this for a second time so the raw edge of the fabric is concealed. pin and then stitch. backstitch at the start and finish to fasten the seam. repeat for the second part circle.

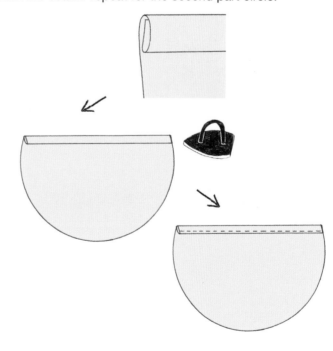

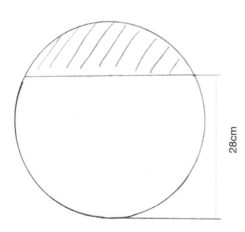

28cm

add the velcro.

these two part circles overlap to complete a full circle; the velcro is fitted to the overlap to create a fastening that keeps the stuffing in place. separate the velcro. on the wrong side of the first part circle, place one half of the velcro strip along the straight edge. pin and stitch. place the second part circle over the first part circle and overlap them so that they create a full circle. place the second half of the velcro strip across the right side of the second part circle so that it lines up with the first velcro strip. pin and stitch. fasten the two velcro edges together to complete the circle and set to one side.

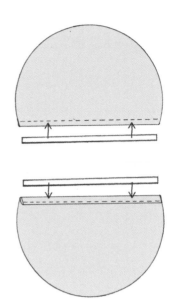

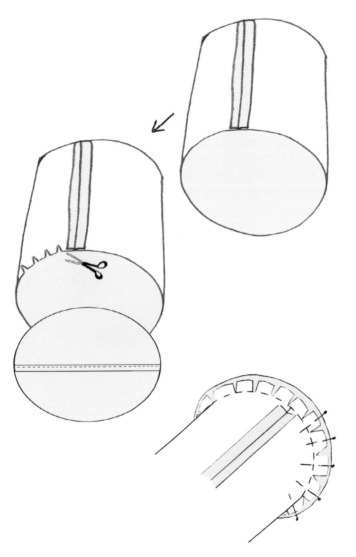

join the side seam.

with right sides facing, place the two short edges of the rectangular lining piece together to create a tube. pin and stitch with a 1.5cm seam allowance. backstitch at the start and finish to fasten the seam. (it is worth double stitching this seam for extra strength.) press the seam open.

fit the end panels.

prepare the main lining piece for fitting the end discs by making a round of 1cm cuts, 2cm apart, at each end. pin the end discs in place. stitch with a 1.5cm seam allowance. (again, it is worth taking the time to double stitch these seams for extra strength.)

prepare the cover.

cut and hem two of the outer fabric discs in the same way as the lining. tack together to make a complete circle. position and tack the piping all the way around the edge of the remaining outer fabric circle, matching the raw edges and neatening the join (see page 21).

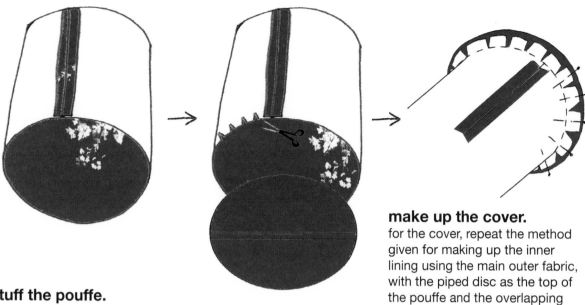

make up the cover.

for the cover, repeat the method given for making up the inner lining using the main outer fabric, with the piped disc as the top of the pouffe and the overlapping part discs as the base.

stuff the pouffe.

turn the main outer cover right side out. insert the inner lining to fit snugly inside with the base openings lined up. fill the pouffe with your chosen stuffing – either fabric scraps or wood shavings until it is firm. fasten the velcro in the lining and overlap the outer fabric cover.

add the buttons.

a very nice decorative touch is to add four buttons to the top of the pouffe. with tailor's chalk, mark four equally spaced points on the top of the pouffe. using a double-ended long upholstery needle, attach the four buttons gathering the fabric up slightly as you sew.

now put your feet up and have a steaming hot cup of tea.

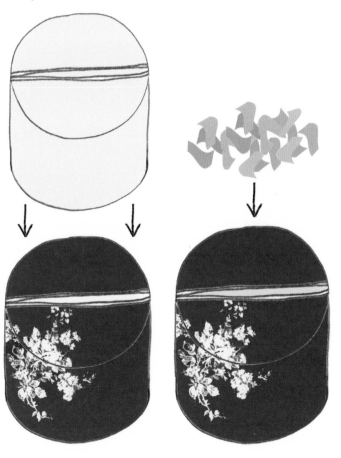

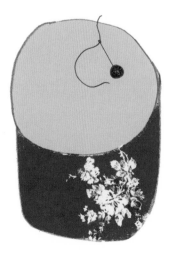

winter curtain.

things you need

- curtain fabric (i recommend heavy weight linen or tasar silk), see 'measure up' for quantity.
- curtain lining fabric (preferably in cream or white), see 'measure up' for quantity.
- 7.5cm pencil header tape.
- brass curtain hooks.
- curtain pole.
- curtain rings (i used painted wooden ones).
- a large, clear space to work and plenty of cups of tea!

curtains can be fantastical and theatrical; the detail and work that goes in to most, from the fabric to their construction, can result in a stunning window dressing. complicated, fiddly components, such as pelmets, frills, weights and other fancy bits, confuse the curtain issue and often scare off the home sewer. however, this winter curtain employs the simplest curtain-making methods i have found and so is designed to be a relatively straightforward make.

for the instructions, i have tried my best to explain every stage in the most direct way possible. the idea is for you to be able to make a functional yet elegant curtain for your home without throwing your sewing machine out of the window in anger. although these curtains are particularly splendid in scale, they are hopefully not too scary to have a go at.

the success of this curtain design lies in the fabric you choose to make it in. matching up repeat patterns on a curtain of this grand a scale is where things start to get really tricky, so if it is your first attempt at sewing curtains, i would take the easiest route. i recommend using a beautifully plain but weighty fabric, such as a tasar silk, and perhaps adding in a panel of a contrasting fabric to add interest.

measure up.

for the main fabric
a pair of curtains or a single curtain?
more often than not, you will need a pair of curtains for a window. however, if your window is 50cm wide or less, a single curtain will be much more suitable, which can be swept to one side when drawn and secured with a complementary tie-back.

width of the curtain
as this is a fairly heavy winter curtain, fit the pole 12cm above the window frame and so that it extends 12cm either side. to achieve a well-fitted curtain, measure the width of the curtain pole and not the window. when using a pencil pleat header tape, as in this case, the width of each curtain in the pair needs to be two and a half times the curtain pole plus a 1cm seam allowance on each side of the width. (for the curtain pictured, i used three panels of fabric per curtain that were stitched together to obtain the required size.)

length of the curtain
i have taken the length of each curtain right to the floor so they 'pool' in a contemporary fashion. this has two benefits: the first is that it looks stylishly modern and the second (more importantly) is that it eliminates any possibility of incorrect measuring and resulting in curtains that are too short! after measuring from the pole to the floor, add an additional 25cm to the length for the curtain's 'pool' and hem.

for the lining fabric
this needs to be 18cm shorter than the main fabric, and 6cm less on the width.

for the header tape
this needs to match the width of the main fabric.

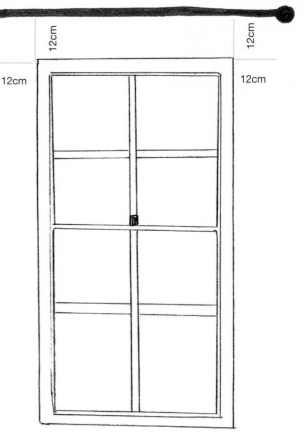

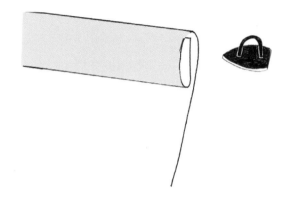

make the curtain panel.

fold a 1cm hem over to the wrong side along the bottom edge of a lining piece and press. repeat to conceal the raw edge. press and pin. stitch the hem. backstitch at the start and finish to fasten the seam. with the lining and main fabric right sides facing, pin together with the top edges meeting. stitch one of the side seams from top to bottom with a 1cm seam allowance. backstitch at the start and finish to fasten the seam. repeat this on the opposite side to make an enormous tube. press the seams open. turn the curtain panel right side out.

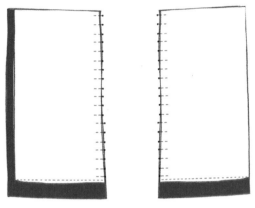

2cm   2cm

press the curtain panel.

with the lining face up, press the curtain panel flat so that the lining is centrally positioned and the excess main fabric is equally divided on either side; there should be approximately a 2cm strip of main fabric at both sides.

1cm

hem the curtain panel.
fold a 1cm hem over to the wrong side along the top of the curtain. flatten the turned edges together, lining to main, so they form a neat straight hem. pin and hand tack the layers together (these tacking stitches will be removed at a later stage).

add the header tape.
position the pencil pleat header tape over the lining 1cm down from the top of the curtain panel and leaving an overhang of 2.5cm at each end. pin in place along the top and bottom edges only of the header tape. if you are making a pair of curtains, at this stage you must work out which is the inner edge of your curtain (the one that will sit in the centre of the window when the curtains are drawn). at the inner edge, on the underside of the overhanging header tape, pull out the cords from the first three slots on both top and bottom edges using your scissors. knot these cords securely together on the wrong side. fold under the header tape so that the knot is hidden and pin in place. on the outer edge, on the top side of the overhanging header tape, pull out the cords as before. knot these cords securely together. (the cords on this side need to be accessible so you can draw them up at a later stage.) fold under the excess header tape pin in place.

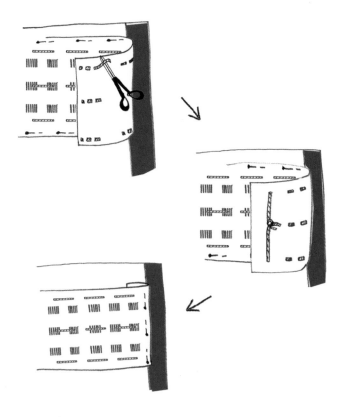

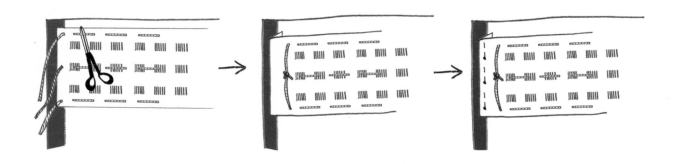

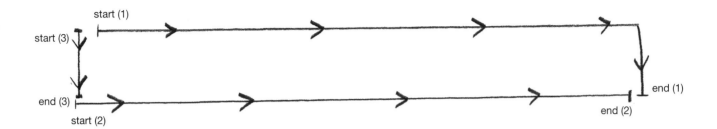

start (1)

start (3)

end (3)

start (2)

end (1)

end (2)

stitch the header tape.

when sewing the header tape in place, you need to keep the curtain absolutely flat and make sure you do not stitch over the cord. the best way to do this is to start at the top left-hand edge, 2.5cm in, and stitch all the way along, stitching as close to the edge as possible for a neat finish. when you reach the end, turn a 90° corner and stitch down the right-hand edge. backstitch at the start and finish to fasten the seam, then cut the thread. starting again at the left-hand edge, stitch the bottom edge of the header tape in the same direction as you stitched the top edge. backstitch at the start and finish to fasten the seam, then cut the thread. stitch the left-hand edge of the header tape securely in place to finish. remove the tacking stitches from the top hem.

1cm

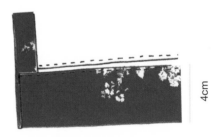

4cm

hem the curtain.

fold a 1cm hem over to the wrong side along the bottom edge of the curtain. fold a further 4cm hem over so the raw edge of the fabric is concealed and press. pin in place and stitch the hem. backstitch at the start and finish to fasten the seam.

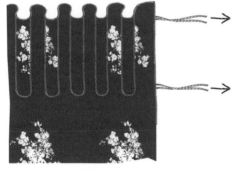

gather the curtain.

to form the pleats simply pull the pre-knotted cord on the header tape until the curtain reaches the desired width. (this should be slightly wider than half the width of the curtain pole, so the pair of curtains meet in the middle when drawn). adjust the pleats so they are neat and uniform. two pairs of hands are useful at this stage, especially if your curtains are on the large size.

fit the hooks.

place the hooks at regular intervals along the header tape. attach the hooks to the prepared curtain rings sitting on your curtain pole.

do it all again.

if you are making a pair, repeat these instructions for the second curtain.

outdoor cushion.

things you need

2 pieces of medium weight linen for the cushion panels, 48cm x 62cm.

2 pieces of medium weight linen for the side panels, 48cm x 7cm.

2 pieces of medium weight linen for the front and back panels, 62cm x 7cm.

1 upholstery zip, 46cm long.

250cm length of contrast piping (optional).

8 buttons (2cm in diameter are ideal).

double-ended upholstery needle.

strong hand-sewing thread.

1 feather-filled box cushion, 46cm x 60cm x 5cm.

whether for a garden bench, patio picnic or pebbly beach, this outdoor cushion is fantastic for lounging around in the summertime. and when it's raining outside, it is also rather handy for indoors too!

fit the zip.

fit the zip to one of the side panels as follows: cut the panel in half lengthwise and fold a 1cm hem over to the wrong side along the length of one side on each piece. press and pin. then follow the instructions for fitting a zip as given on pages 22–3.

make the gusset.

close the zip fitted in the side panel. with the right sides facing, pin the ends of the two side panels to each end of the back panel so the raw edges meet. stitch together leaving a 1cm seam allowance. back stitch at the start and finish to fasten the seam. press the seams open. repeat this to join the front panel to the other ends of the side panels, pressing the seams open once sewn. you should end up with a floppy rectangle shape, which is the cushion gusset.

add the piping.

if you are adding piping (as i have done in the cushion pictured), tack this in place all the way around the edge of the bottom and top cushion pieces. follow the instructions for adding piping as given on page 21.

join the top and bottom pieces.

with the right sides together, pin the gusset to the bottom cushion piece. i find it easier to start with the zip panel and work my way round, pinning as i go and making sure the seams meet as planned in the corners. follow the instructions for sewing box corners as given on page 18. stitch the gusset in place with one continuous seam, leaving a 1cm seam allowance. backstitch at the start and finish to fasten the seam. (make sure the zip is open for the next bit as you will need to get a hand in to turn the cushion cover right side out once you have finished stitching.) repeat this process to join the gusset to the top cushion piece. turn the cover right side out and press the seams (the edge of the ironing board helps with this).

stuff the cushion.

fill the cover with the feather-filled cushion pad, making sure it neatly fills all four corners.

add the buttons.

this next bit is rather fiddly. you will need a little patience and, at times, some brute force! with tailor's chalk, mark four equally spaced points on the top of the cushion. thread your double-ended long upholstery needle with a good metre of thread. secure the thread to the first marked point with a few backstitches. push the needle right the way through the cushion to the under side and pull the thread through. fasten the thread up and back through the first button. push the needle back through the cushion right next to the point at which you came through previously. push the needle back through to the side you started with and pull as tight as you can so the button on the opposite side makes a neat, firm indentation. the tricky bit here is to keep the first button firmly in place while you push the thread up and back through the second button in order to make the same indentation on this side. you then have to do a bit of a patient poking trick to push the needle through the buttonholes so as to stitch the two buttons together with the cushion pad sandwiched in between, making the double dimple effect. when you have managed to stitch too and fro through both buttons four of five times, fasten the stitch with a number of small backstitches underneath the first button. secure with a knot, then trim the thread and wind any excess thread around the button. repeat this for the remaining three double dimples.

after all that, i suggest relaxing in the garden on the finished cushion with a freshly made glass of pimms!

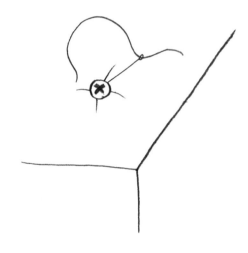

for the **bedroom**

piped cushion.

things you need

1 large sheet of paper or newspaper, at least 50cm x 50cm

pencil and a length of string

2 discs of medium weight cotton, 48cm in diameter.

1 upholstery zip, 48cm long.

1 feather-filled round cushion pad, 46cm in diameter.

a length of contrast piping, slightly less than 2m long.

a swish touch to any cushion, piping is less tricky than you may think to attach and, with a bit of practice, can take a simple cushion to a new level. i have used a complimentary off-white colour here, but piping can work really well indeed when highly contrasted to frame a beautiful printed fabric. i have shown both a round and square cushion here; the two shapes are equal in terms of effort and very similar in their methods of construction.

make the template.

the best way to do this is to use the old trick of attaching a piece of string to a pencil. measure the length of string to 24cm (half the diameter of the circle 48cm required). with one hand, hold the end of the string in the centre of the sheet of paper and with the other hand pull the string taught. draw the pencil round to create a full circle. cut out this paper pattern and then use it as a template to cut out the two circles of fabric needed.

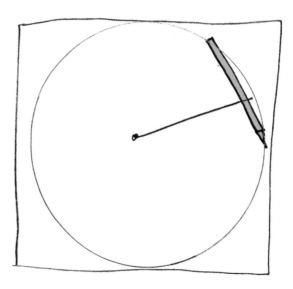

add the piping.
on the right side of the first fabric disc, pin and tack the piping in place all the way around the edge of the circle. follow the instructions for adding piping as given on page 21.

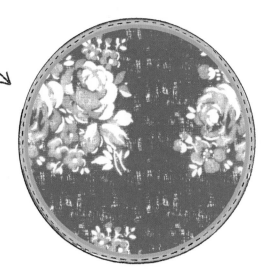

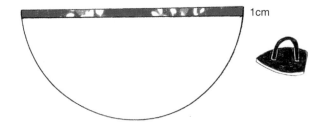

1cm

fit the zip.
cut the second disc in half directly down the middle. fold a 1cm hem over to the wrong side along both straight edges. press and pin. then follow the instructions for fitting a zip as given on pages 22–3.

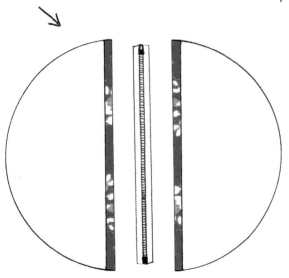

join the panels.

with right sides facing, place the two prepared circles together so the raw edges meet. unzip the zip to over half way so you will be able to turn the cover right side out once stitched. pin and stitch all the way around. the foot of the machine should sit just on the right-hand side of the piping so that you stitch the piping tightly and neatly in place. if you are finding it tricky, take your time and have a few practice goes on some waste fabric until you have got the hang of it. alternatively, if you have a very flashy sewing machine you may have a special piping foot which will help no end. this is not essential, however, i always attach piping with either a regular or zip foot.

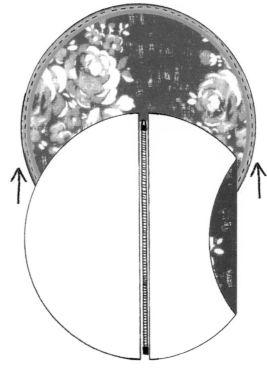

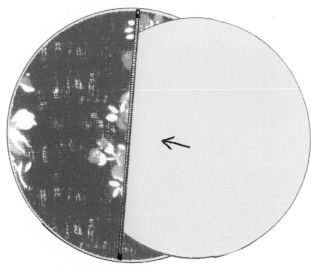

stuff the cushion.

turn the cushion cover right side out. stuff with cushion pad.

for a square cushion

this method translates fairly easily over all shapes of cushion, from square, rectangular and even triangular if you fancy! it is just a little trickier on the sharper corners, but as long as you tack the piping in place first and give the corners a bit of extra time and concentration it should be trouble-free. and like everything in life, practice makes perfect!

hot-water bottle cover.

things you need

medium weight cotton (i have recycled an old soft cotton curtain) for the main body, cut to size (see template on page 142 – cut 1 front piece and 2 back pieces).

4oz polyester wadding, cut 2cm smaller than the main body all the way round (see template on page 142 – cut 1 front piece and 2 back pieces).

light weight fabric (cotton calico is ideal) for the lining, cut to the size (see template on page 142 – cut 1 front piece and 2 back pieces).

1m length of bias binding (2.5cm wide)

nestling under the duvet on a chilly winter's night with a great book, a mug of cocoa and a hot-water bottle to toast your feet... what more could a girl want in life?

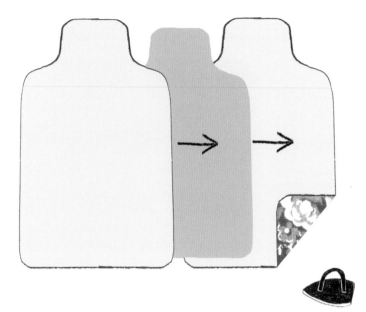

bond the panels and wadding.

lay the front outer fabric piece right side down on the ironing board. lay the front wadding piece on top and then the front lining piece on top of that, rather like making a sandwich. with a hot iron, press the sandwich pile so it flattens the wadding slightly and loosely bonds the three layers together. repeat for the two back pieces.

add the bias binding.

cut two lengths of bias binding to slightly longer than the width of the back pieces. fold these pieces of bias binding in half lengthwise. slot one binding strip onto each of the straight edges of the back pieces. pin in place. stitch the bias binding in place, trapping all three layers neatly together. backstitch at the start and finish to fasten the seam.

join the panels.

with right sides facing, lay the top back panel on to the front panel so the top edges line up. then lay the bottom back panel on top of this so the two back panels overlap in the middle and the bottom edges of the back and front panels line up. pin in place through all the layers. starting at the bottom edge, stitch all the way with a 2cm seam allowance. for extra strength, backstitch a couple of times when sewing over the bound edges of the top and bottom back panels. backstitch at the start and finish to fasten the seam.

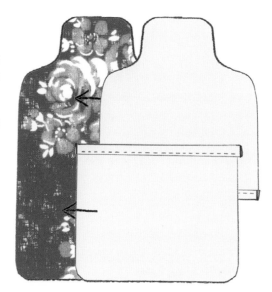

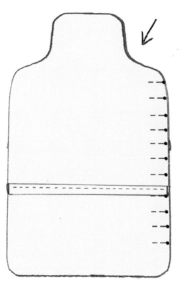

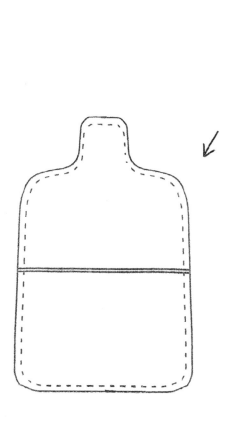

fill the cover with the hottie.

turn the hot-water bottle cover right side out, pushing out all the corners. boil the kettle, fill your hot-water bottle and slip it into the cover.

toasty!

appliquéd cushion.

things you need

2 circles of medium weight fabric (i have used linen here) for the cushion base, 52cm in diameter (see page 93 for drawing and cutting out).

a selection of patterned or coloured fabrics for the appliqué.

1 feather-filled round cushion pad, 50cm in diameter.

1 sheet of bondaweb fusible webbing (widely available from good haberdashers).

fabric crayons (optional).

1 upholstery zip, 50cm long.

scrap cotton to use when ironing.

this project is aimed at the more artistically minded maker – let your creative juices run riot and create your own fabric 'collage'. for the cushion shown here, i combined appliqué with a freehand drawing in fabric crayons, which are a wonderful way to doodle on to fabric. the crayons are permanently fixed by a hot iron so they bake on to the fabric. i love the naïve quality of the drawn line combined with the intricate pattern of the vintage fabric. of course you can simply use appliqué and the lines of your stitching to create a design. even a stripe or spot appliqué in a patterned fabric looks very effective.

sketch your design.

this is where your own creativity comes to the fore. once you have settled on your design, the appliqué part can be as simple or as complex as you like. if you are combining appliqué with a crayon drawing this needs to be drawn and fixed to the fabric first. if you are not 100% confident in drawing freehand directly onto the fabric then practise on a sheet of paper. make sure you draw with a heavy line so the drawing can be placed underneath the fabric and the drawing traced directly from it. if you are struggling to see through the fabric, tape the paper drawing to a window and lay the fabric on top – the light from the window will help. trace your design with fabric crayons on to the fabric. fix the crayon drawing with a hot iron following the instructions on the pack.

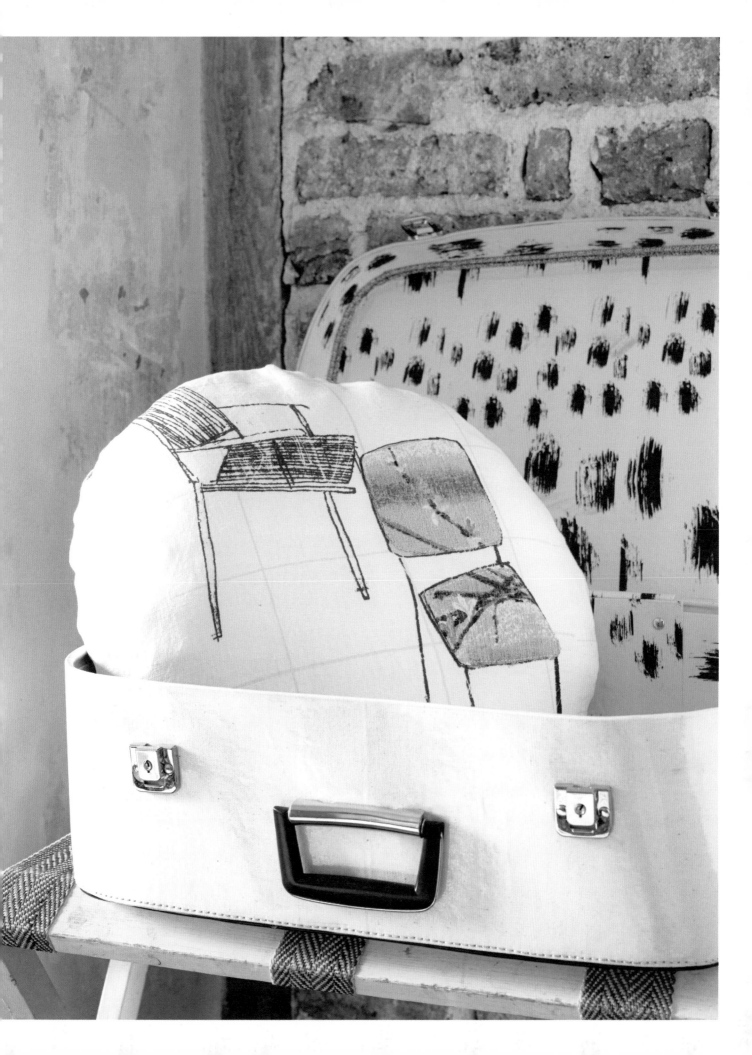

cut out the appliqué.

when you have decided on the shape of the appliqué
motifs, draw them onto paper and cut out. place them
face down on the paper side of the bondaweb. cut out
roughly, then iron onto the wrong side of the patterned
fabric, following the instructions on the packet (these
do vary slightly from brand to brand). i always lay some
scrap cotton on top to protect my iron when pressing
the shapes. cut the shapes out around your pencil lines
and peel off the bondaweb backing. position these in
the desired place on your cushion front. press with a hot
iron to bond together.

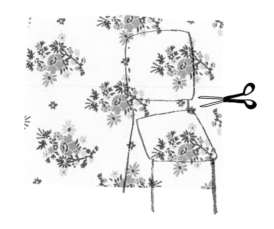

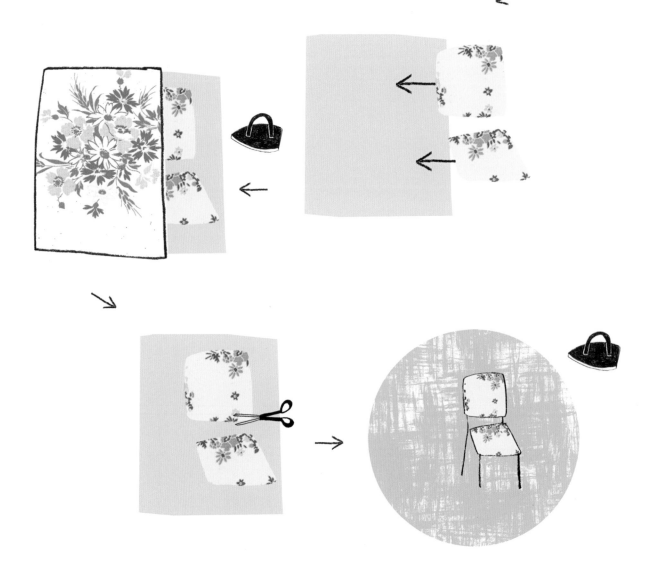

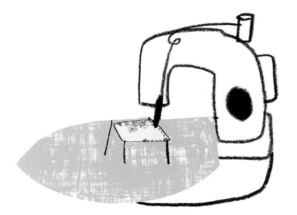

add the appliqué.

each bonded appliqué motif must be firmly stitched in place before sewing up the cushion cover. using either a contrast colour thread or one matched to the colour of the appliqué, carefully stitch around each shape. stitch as close to the edges as possible for a neat finish. backstitch at the start and finish to fasten.

fit the zip.

cut the second circle in half directly down the middle. fold a 1cm hem over to the wrong side along both straight edges. press and pin. then follow the instructions for fitting a zip as given on pages 22–3.

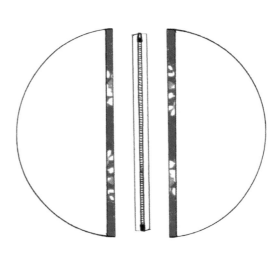

1cm

join the panels.

with right sides facing, place the two prepared circles together so the raw edges meet. unzip the zip to over half way so you will be able to turn the cover right side out once stitched. pin and stitch all the way around with a 1cm seam allowance. backstitch at the start and finish to secure the seam. trim the excess seam allowance with pinking shears and turn the cushion cover out to the right side and press. stuff with the feather cushion pad.

done!

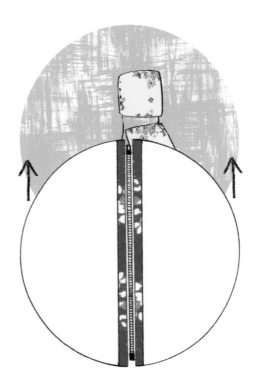

hanger coats.

things you need

2 pieces of light or medium weight cotton or silk, cut to size (see template on page 142).

1 wire coat hanger.

there is nothing more infuriating than a tangle of wire coat hangers. besides, they are not the best things in the wardrobe to look after your favourite silk dresses. these easy to make but extremely functional and rather attractive mini coats for those troublesome wire hangers will have your wardrobe organised and stylishly chic in no time. they are also a great way to use up odds and ends of vintage fabric!

hem the panels.

turn 5mm over to the wrong side along the straight edge and press. repeat this for a second time so the raw edge of the fabric is concealed. pin in place. repeat this for the second panel. stitch the pressed hems, stitching as close to the inside edge of the turned hem as possible for a neat finish. backstitch at the start and finish to fasten the seam.

join the panels.

with right sides facing, place the two pieces together so the two hemmed edges meet. starting at the hemmed base, stitch from a to b. backstitch at the start and finish to fasten the seam. then stitch from c to d. again backstitch at the start and finish to fasten the seam.

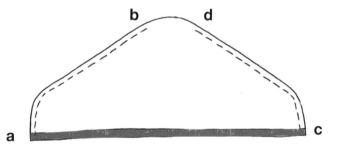

add the hanger.

turn the hanger coat out to the right side and press. fit the coat over the wire hanger, taking the hanger's 'neck' through the hole at the top. hand stitch the hole at the top with a couple of extra stitches to secure.

suit carrier.

things you need

oilcloth fabric, 150cm x 150cm will be plenty, cut to size (see template on page 141 – cut 2 pieces).

1 upholstery zip, 110cm long.

1 piece of cotton fabric for the zip end, 3cm x 4cm or thereabouts.

1 wire coat hanger (ideally with hanger coat, see page 105).

1 piece of cotton for loop, 4cm x 10cm or thereabouts.

3m length of bias binding, 2.5cm wide.

are you tired of travelling with smart outfits squished into your suitcase, making them creased and crumpled? well this very easy to make suit carrier not only holds suits but also coats, dresses, blouses and posh sweaters too! even when you aren't going anywhere, it is a great way of protecting your favourite clothes while they are hanging in the wardrobe.

make the loop.

fold a 1cm hem over to the wrong side along each long edge of the fabric piece and press. then fold the fabric down the middle lengthwise so the two turned edges meet. press and pin. stitch along the open side, stitching as close to the edge as possible for a neat finish. backstitch at the start and finish to fasten the seam. stitch the same line along the opposite side to finish the loop.

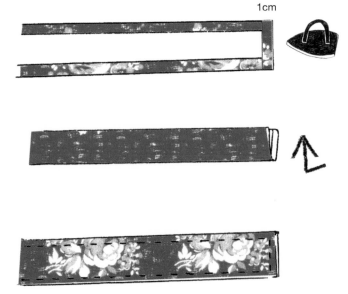

1cm

add the bias binding.
fold the front piece in half widthways and cut along this line. fold the bias binding in half lengthwise and press. starting on the straight edge, pin the bias binding all the way round the first front half. follow the instructions for adding biad binding as given on page 20. repeat this on the corresponding straight edge of the second half.

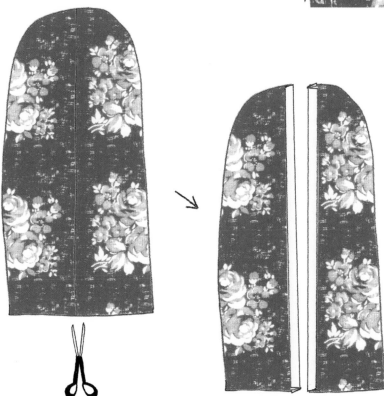

add the zip end.
before fitting the zip, add the zip end. place the small zip end piece and the cut end of the zip right sides together. stitch in place with a 5mm hem. fold the unstitched side of the zip end back 1cm, then fold the whole piece around to the back side of the zip being careful to keep the raw edge tucked underneath. stitch in place sewing a little to the right of the first seam just sewn, making sure to catch the tucked side of the zip end in as you stitch.

fit the zip.

fit the zip to the two front panels: the open end of the zip needs to start at the top of the suit carrier and should line up with the top of the bound edge. pin the zip in place along each edge in turn. the zip should finish 10cm short of the bottom edge. then follow the instructions for fitting a zip as given on page 23.

join the panels.

with right sides facing, place the front and back panels together so the raw edges meet. the two pieces of oilcloth may stick together so it can take some time to line them up exactly. unzip the zip to over half way so you will be able to turn the cover right side out once stitched. pin all the way round. fold your prepared loop in half widthways. then slot it in between the front and back panels at the centre of the bottom edge, with the fold facing inwards and the raw edges lining up. pin in place. stitch around the outside edge with a 2cm seam allowance, trapping in the loop as you sew. backstitch at the start and finish to fasten the seam. trim the excess seam allowance all the way round with pinking shears.

add the hanger.

turn the suit carrier out to the right side. fit the suit carrier over the wire hanger, taking the hanger's 'neck' through the hole at the top where the zip finishes.

now fill the carrier with your best outfits. i highly recommend taking a weekend away to test your new suit carrier fully!

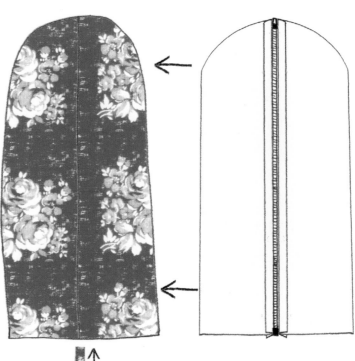

pin tucked cushion

things you need

1 large sheet of paper or newspaper, at least 50cm x 50cm.

pencil and a length of string.

1 piece of medium-weight cotton, 50cm x 150cm, for front panel.

1 circle of medium-weight canvas or cotton drill, 50cm in diameter, for back panel.

1 upholstery zip, 50cm long.

cotton for zip end, 3cm x 4cm.

tailor's chalk.

pin tucking is a straightforward sewing technique, which delivers stunningly elegant results. it is a rather lengthy process, but once you have the hang of pin tucking, it is both simple and satisifying.

you can achieve countless variations in size, scale and texture when you vary the width of the pin tucks and weight of the fabric. the lighter the weight of the fabric, the smaller the pin tucks can go, whilst larger, bolder, textured pin tucks can be achieved with wonderful weighty linens and vintage cottons. here I have used a tasar silk with a beautiful sheen to it, which is nice and sturdy to work with and produces a bold and gloriously textured result.

make the template.

the best way to do this is to use the old trick of attaching a piece of string to a pencil. measure the length of string to 25cm (half the diameter of the circle 50cm required). with one hand, hold the end of the string in the centre of the sheet of paper and with the other hand pull the string taught. draw the pencil round to create a full circle. cut out the template and put it to one side – it will be used later to cut out the circular panels.

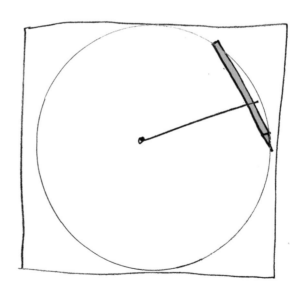

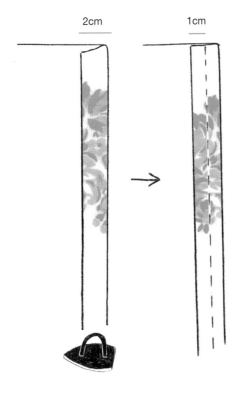

2cm   1cm

make the pin tucked panel.

you will need your iron and ironing board set up as near as possible to your sewing machine. starting at the left edge of the front panel piece, fold the fabric over by 2cm and press. stitch a 1cm hem down the length of the fold. press the seam flat on the back and front and press the pin tuck to the left. (one down lots to go!) measuring from the newly stitched line, fold the fabric again by 2cm and press. stitch a 1cm hem down the length of the fold. press this on the back and front, pressing the pin tuck to the left. repeat this all the way along the fabric until you have pin tucked the lot. this takes a little time, too-ing and fro-ing from sewing machine to iron, but I actually find it quite therapeutic.

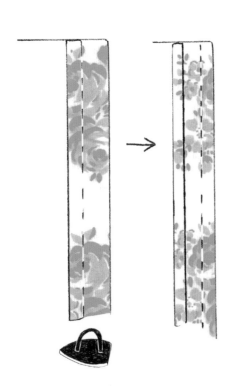

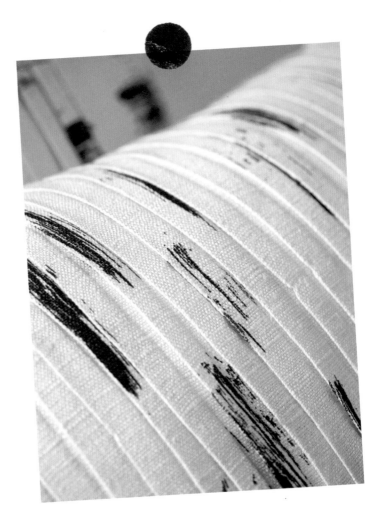

fit the zip.

cut the back panel in half directly down the middle. fold 1cm hem over to the wrong side along both newly cut straight edges. press and pin. then follow the instructions for fitting a zip as given on page 23.

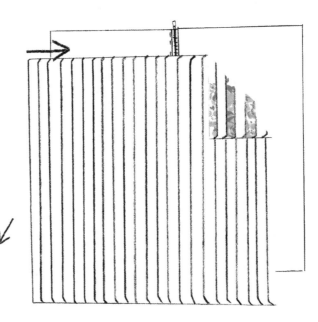

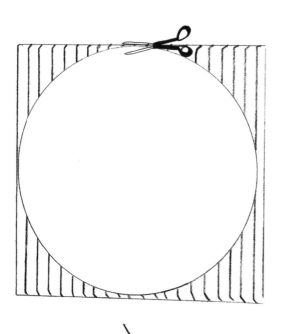

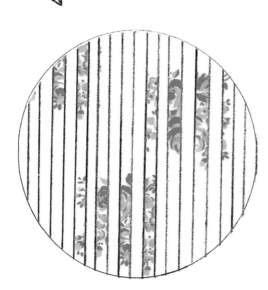

join the panels.

with right sides facing, place the front and back panels together so the raw edges meet. place the circular template on top and, using tailor's chalk, trace around the template on to the fabric. unzip the zip to over half way so you will be able to turn the cover right side out once stitched. pin the panels together all the way round just inside the chalk line. cut out following the chalk line. stitch all the way round with a 1cm seam allowance. backstitch at the start and finish to fasten the seam. to neaten a curved seam, cut notches into the seam allowance. turn the cushion cover out to the right side out and press. stuff with the feather cushion pad.

note.

it is nice to vary the pin tucking here and there. it works very well if you pin tuck only two thirds of the front panel leaving a flat area which is 'un-tucked', as I have done on the round cushion shown on page 110. otherwise, if you prefer a square or rectangular cushion, sew straight seams instead of curved.

bedspread.

things you need

2 pieces of dupion silk, each measuring 137cm x 200cm

1 piece of 6oz polyester wadding, 137cm x 200cm (you may have to use 2 pieces to achieve this size)

linen for the edging, 2 pieces measuring 24cm x 204cm and a further 2 pieces measuring 24cm x 141cm

tailor's chalk and metre rule (optional).

snuggling up with a hot chocolate and the sunday newspapers is a wonderful (albeit rather rare) luxury. in the winter months, layering an extra bedspread on top of a duvet or traditional sheets provides much-needed extra warmth to a bed and achieves that snug-as-a-bug-in-a-rug feeling!

draw out the grid.

you will need a large floor area or table to work on for this project: it is not difficult, but it does take up a rather large space! with wrong sides facing, lay the two silk pieces on top of each other with the wadding sandwiched in between. the idea is to stitch a 10cm grid all over the bedspread. this can either be sewn 'by eye' creating an endearingly naïve look (one which i personally love) or for greater accuracy you can draw straight lines onto the fabric using tailor's chalk and a metre ruler as a guide.

stitch the grid.

hand tack all three layers together with
lines of stitching 10cm apart, running
lengthwise down the fabric. stitch along
the rows. backstitch at the start and
finish to fasten the lines of stitching.
turn the bedspread 90 degrees. hand
tack lines of stitching 10cm apart,
running all the way across the fabric,
to complete the grid. stitch along the
rows. backstitch at the start and finish to
fasten the lines of stitching. (see page
12 for more information on tacking and
stitching.) if you find the bulk of three
layers of fabric too great to fit under the
arm of your sewing machine, the layers
can be stitched together by hand.

10cm

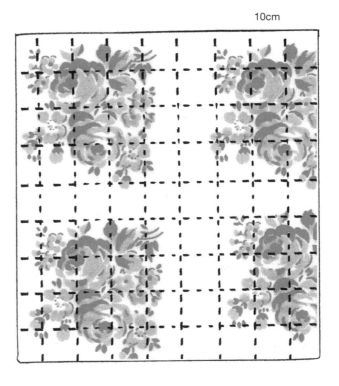

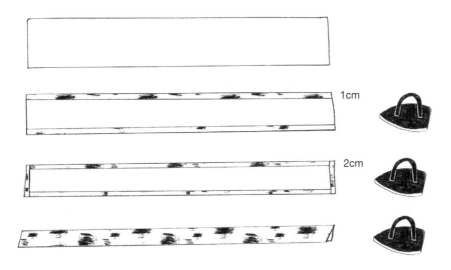

1cm

2cm

prepare the edging.

fold a 1cm hem over to
the wrong side along each
long edge of the edging
pieces and press. fold
a 2cm hem over to the
wrong side at both short
ends and press. then
fold each piece down the
middle lengthwise so the
two turned edges meet.
press and pin.

edge the bedspread.

starting with the two longest edges, sandwich the stitched bedspread panel into a folded edging piece, one on either side. pin in place and stitch. stitch as close to the edges as possible for a neat finish. backstitch at the start and finish to fasten.

finish the bedspread.

repeat this along the two shorter edges. overlap the longer edge pieces at the corners. pin in place and stitch as before, but this time turn under each end for a neat finish. backstitch at the start and finish to fasten the seam.

fling the finished bedspread onto your freshly laundered bed. add cushions, maybe the daily newspaper and relax!

for the laundry

laundry or storage bag.

things you need

1 piece of medium weight cotton or linen (I have used a medium weight plain weave cotton), measuring 150cm x 60cm.

2 lengths of cotton cord, each 120cm long, for drawstring ties.

1 large safety or nappy pin.

keep your dirty laundry in order until wash day in a fabulous handmade bag. it is also extremely useful for storing a million other things – shoe polish, babies' bits and pieces, soap flakes, socks and undies...

the instructions here are for a laundry bag, but using this method you can make a bag to any size you like depending what you need it for. simply scale the measurements given either up or down proportionally.

prepare the cord casing.

measure 8cm in from each end of the fabric piece and make a cut of 1cm at each corner as shown to create a flap.

stitch the cord casing.

fold each cord casing flap over to the wrong side by 5mm. press. fold again by a further 5mm to enclose the raw edge. press. pin and stitch. backstitch at the start and finish to fasten the seam.

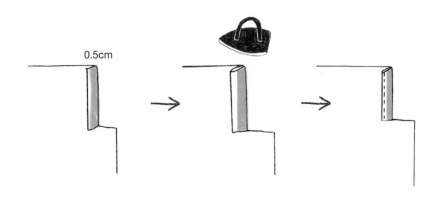

finish the cord casing.

fold a 1cm hem over to the wrong side along each short end. press. then fold the short edges over to the wrong side again so they are level with the previous 1cm cut made in the fabric. press. pin and stitch in place. stitch as close to the edges as possible for a neat finish. backstitch at the start and finish to fasten.

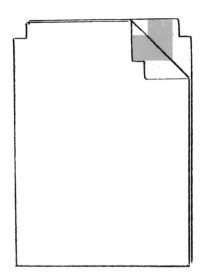
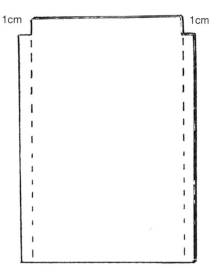

stitch the bag.

with right sides facing, fold the whole fabric piece in half so the raw edges meet as shown. pin the side edges together. stitch both edges with a 1cm seam allowance. trim the excess seam allowance all the way round with pinking shears.

finish the bag.

turn the bag right side out and press the seams. cut the cotton cord in half and attach the end of each piece to a large safety pin (if you can get your hands on one, old-fashioned nappy pins are best for this). thread the two cords all the way through both sides of the cord casing. when fully threaded, and holding onto both ends of the cords, gently pull one of the ends to determine which cord is which, and fasten each cord separately with a secure knot. to finish pull one of the knotted cords through to the opposite side of the casing so you end up with a knot at either side, making it super easy to draw the strings together when you need to close the bag.

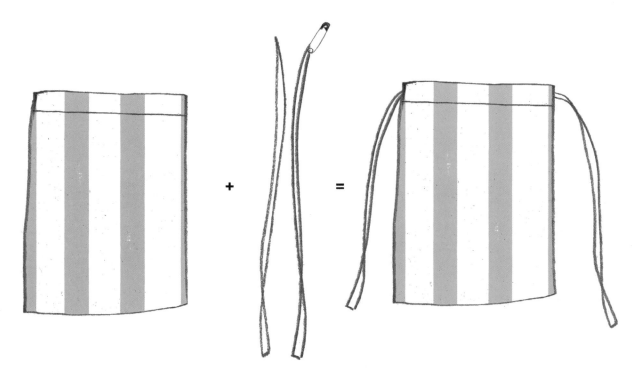

peg bag.

things you need

1 piece of medium weight cotton canvas, measuring 40cm x 80cm.

2 lengths of bias binding, each 50cm long.

2 lengths of cotton cord, each 20cm long, for ties.

1 length of square wooden dowel, 1.8cm x 1.8cm x 38cm.

1 metal screw hook (one taken from an old wooden coat hanger is ideal).

"we're going to hang out the washing on the siegfried line"... why not do it in style with a home-made peg bag. a lovely stripe or super bright floral print fabric with contrast binding works excellently for this project. wooden pegs are a must-have!

add the bias binding and ties.
fold each strip of bias binding lengthwise and pin in place over the short edges of the canvas. with the fabric face up, at the centre of each bound edge slot a cord tie underneath the bias binding. pin in place. stitch as close to the turned edge of the binding as possible, taking care to catch the underside of the binding as you sew and to secure the ties; for extra strength make a double stitch over each tie. tuck the raw edge of the binding under for a neat finish at each end.

sew the side seams.
with right sides facing, fold the canvas so the bound edges meet one third of the way down from the top. pin and stitch the side seams with a 1cm seam allowance. backstitch the start and finish to fasten the seam.

add the hook and dowel.
turn the peg bag right side out and press. slot the dowel into the top of the bag to fit snugly. with tailor's chalk, mark the centre point along the top edge. screw the hook into the dowel through the fabric at this point.

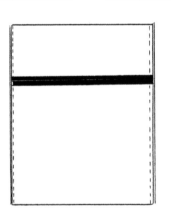

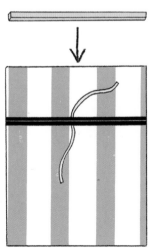

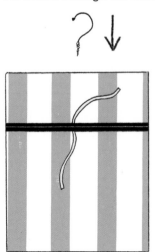

the peg bag is now ready to fill with pegs!

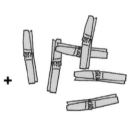

carrier bag holder.

things you need

1 piece of medium weight cotton or linen, measuring 40cm x 62cm.

1 disc of medium weight cotton or linen, 14cm in diameter, for base.

1 length of cotton cord, 100cm long, for drawstring ties.

2 lengths of bias binding, each 16cm long.

do your bit for the environment by making sure you recycle any carrier bags that you pick up on shopping trips. this snazzy home-made holder keeps plastic bags neat, tidy and ready to reuse.

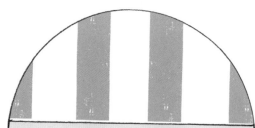
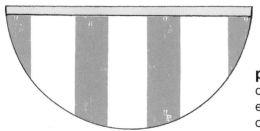

prepare the base.

cut the cotton disc in half directly down the middle. fold each strip of bias binding lengthwise and pin in place over the straight edges. stitch as close to the turned edge of the binding as possible, taking care to catch the underside of the binding as you sew. tuck the raw edge of the binding under for a neat finish at each end.

prepare the cord casing.

measure 8cm in from one end of the fabric piece and make a cut of 1cm at both corners as shown to create a flap.

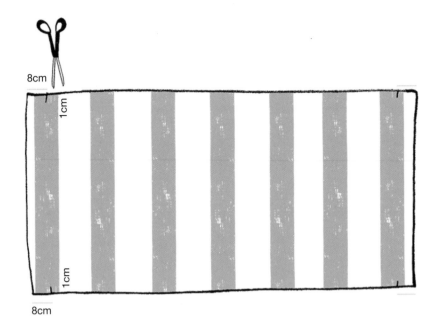

8cm
1cm
1cm
8cm

stitch the cord casing.

fold each cord casing flap over to the wrong side by 5mm. press. fold again by a further 5mm to enclose the raw edge. press. pin and stitch. backstitch at the start and finish to fasten the seam.

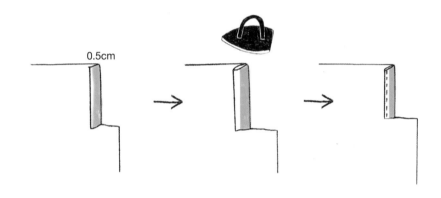

0.5cm

1cm

finish the cord casing.

fold a 1cm hem over to the wrong side along each short end. press. then fold the short edges over to the wrong side again so they are level with the previous 1cm cut made in the fabric. press. pin and stitch in place. stitch as close to the edges as possible for a neat finish. backstitch at the start and finish to fasten.

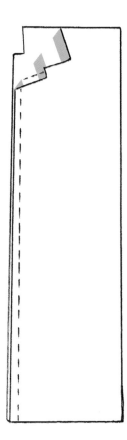

stitch the holder.
with right sides facing, fold the whole fabric piece in half lengthwise so the raw edges meet as shown. pin the edges together. stitch the side seam with a 1cm seam allowance.

fit the base.
prepare the main piece for fitting the base by making a round of 1cm cuts, 2cm apart, at each end. with the bound edges of the two base pieces butted up together, pin the base in place. stitch with a 1.5cm seam allowance. this is a little tricky so take your time: if you need to add a little pleat here and there to make it fit, then do. backstitch at the start and finish to fasten the stitch.

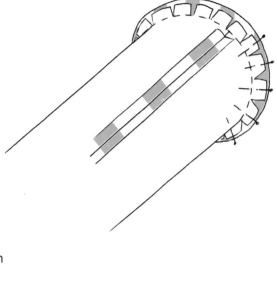

finish the holder.
turn the bag right side out and press the seams. cut the cotton cord in half and attach the end of each piece to a large safety or nappy pin. thread the two cords all the way through both sides of the cord casing. when fully threaded, and holding onto both ends of the cords, gently pull one of the ends to determine which cord is which, and fasten each cord separately with a secure knot. to finish pull one of the knotted cords through to the opposite side of the casing so you end up with a knot at either side, making it super easy to draw the strings together when you need to close the holder.

now fill your holder with carrier bags!

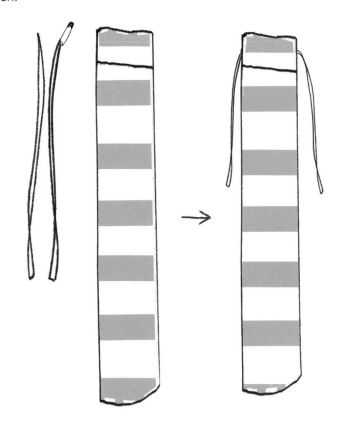

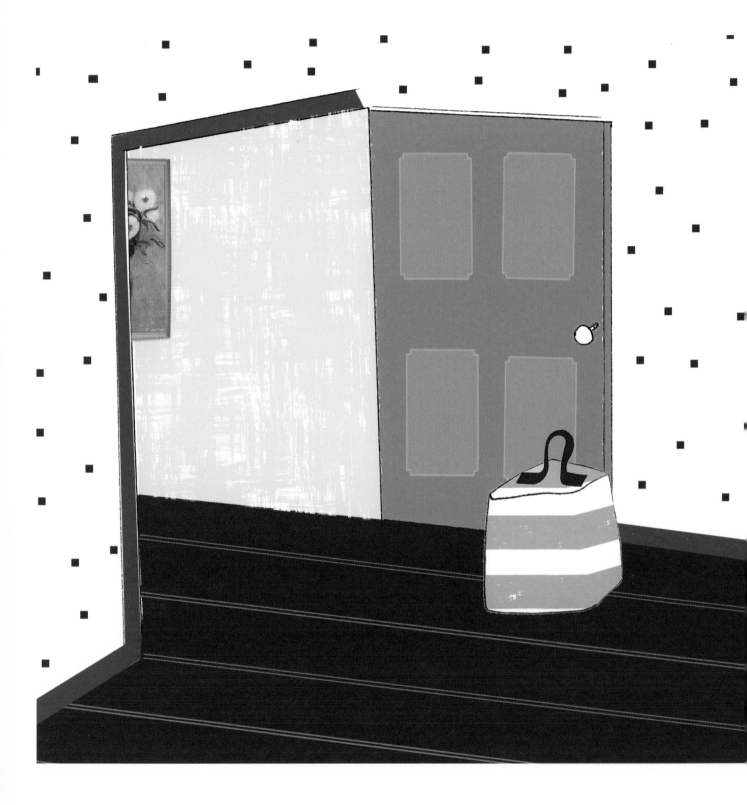

door stop.

things you need

2 pieces of medium or heavy weight cotton, 16cm x 16cm, for the base and lid.

1 piece of medium or heavy weight cotton, 62cm x 20cm, for the main body.

1 piece or medium or heavy weight cotton, 22cm x 6cm, for the handle.

1 large plastic freezer bag or similar.

1 elastic band.

a small amount of sand, rice or similar for filling.

this handy little door stop, in all its home-made glory, is a classic design; simple to make, it will prevent your doors from slamming. a medium to heavy weight cotton is the best fabric to use for this project.

make the handle.
fold a 1cm hem over to the wrong side along all four sides of the fabric piece and press. then fold the fabric down the middle lengthwise so the turned edges meet. press and pin. stitch together all the way around, stitching as close to the edge as possible for a neat finish. backstitch at the start and finish to fasten the seam.

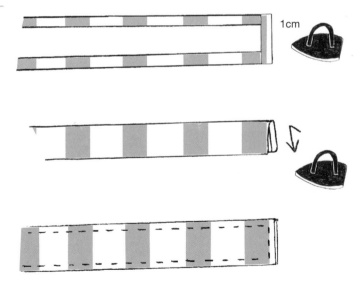

add the handle.

on the right side of the lid piece position the ends of the handle as shown. pin in place. stitch the handle to the door stop lid; for extra strength stitch a rectangle and then add a cross in the middle.

fit the zip.

cut the base piece in half directly down the middle. fold a 1cm hem over to the wrong side along both newly cut edges. press and pin. then follow the instructions for fitting a zip as given on page 23. put to one side.

stitch the body.

with right sides facing, fold the main body in half widthways so the raw edges meet as shown. pin the edges together. stitch the side seam with a 1cm seam allowance. press the seam flat.

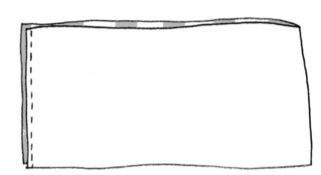

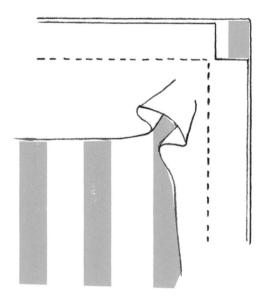

join all the pieces.
with the right sides facing, pin the main body to the base piece. clip the corner to achieve a neat finish. (make sure the zip is open for the next bit as you will need to get a hand in to turn the door stop right side out once you have finished stitching.) following the instructions for sewing box corners as given on page 18, stitch the main body in place with one continuous seam, leaving a 1cm seam allowance. backstitch at the start and finish to fasten the seam. repeat this process to join the main body to the lid piece. turn the door stop right side out and press the seams (the edge of the ironing board helps with this).

line and fill the door stop.
line the door stop with the plastic freezer bag. fill the bag with sand, rice or other chosen filling; during filling, give the door stop a few vigorous shakes to ensure it is filled to its maximum. twist the opening of the plastic bag together and secure with an elastic band. zip up the door stop and it is ready to use.

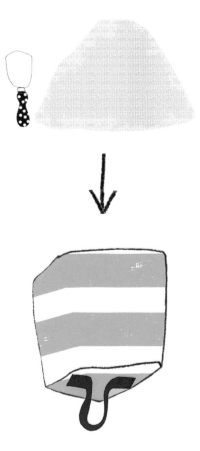

shoe bag.

things you need

2 pieces of medium weight cotton, 38cm x 46cm.

1 piece of medium weight cotton, 24cm x 12cm.

1 closed zip, 40cm long.

i find these little shoe bags extremely useful, especially when travelling. they are great for when you need to pack shows into your suitcase, neatly and cleanly protecting both your shoes and your clothes. they are also great for popping trainers into, whether for a game of tennis or a jog after work!

make the loop.

fold a 1cm hem over to the wrong side along all four sides of the fabric piece and press. then fold the fabric down the middle lengthwise so the turned edges meet. press and pin. stitch together all the way round, stitching as close to the edge as possible for a neat finish. backstitch at the start and finish to fasten the seam.

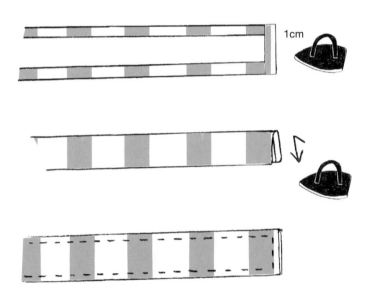

1cm

fit the zip.

fold a 1cm hem over to the wrong side along one short end of both the two main cotton pieces. press and pin. then follow the instructions for fitting a zip as given on page 23. trim any excess seam allowance with pinking shears.

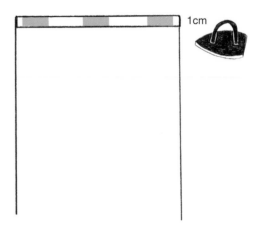

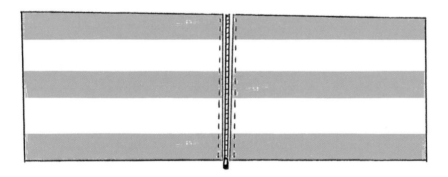

stitch the bag.

pin the other two short edges together, with right sides facing. stitch with a 1cm seam allowance. press the seam flat. turn the bag out to the right side. (the bag is finished with french seams along the sides, so there is no danger of fluffing your suede shoes with any raw fabric edges inside). then position the bag so that the zip sits 8cm down from the top edge and so the raw edges meet as shown. pin the edges together. stitch the side seams with a 1cm seam allowance, making sure the zip is half open. trim the seam allowance back to 5mm. turn the bag back to the wrong side.

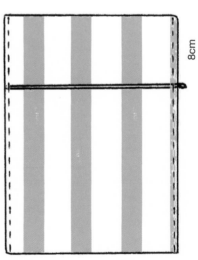

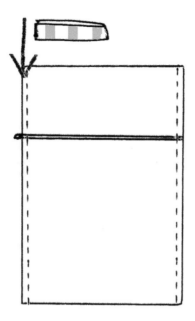

add the loop.

with the bag wrong side out and the zipped front face up, tuck the folded loop inside the bag at the top left hand corner so the raw edges of the loop butt up to the inside seam. pin in place. then stitch down each side with a 1.5cm seam allowance, enclosing the raw edges into the french seam as you sew (see page 17), taking care to secure the loop; for extra strength make a double stitch over the loop. turn the bag out to the right side and press to finish.

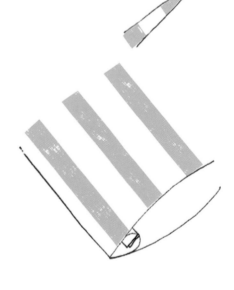

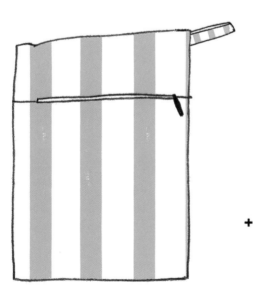

+

templates.

not to scale. each
square of the each grid
represents 5cm x 5cm.

egg cosy (see pages 38–9).

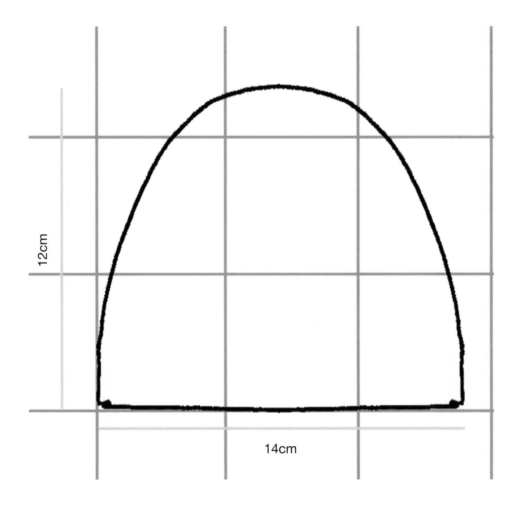

12cm

14cm

apron (see pages 40–1).

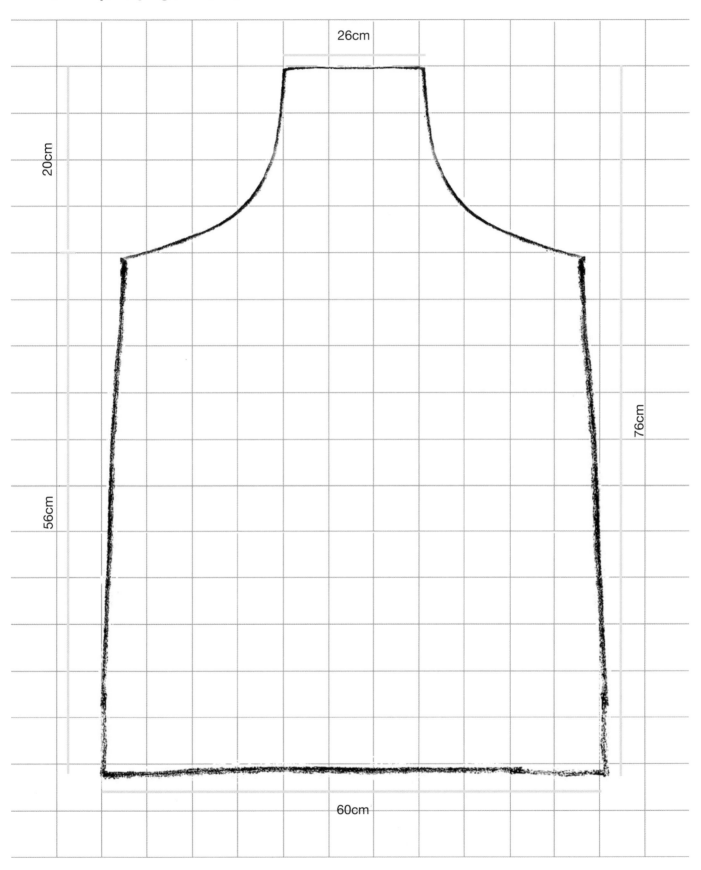

26cm

20cm

76cm

56cm

60cm

**hanger coat
(see pages 104–5).**

14cm

42cm

**suit carrier
(see pages 106–9).**

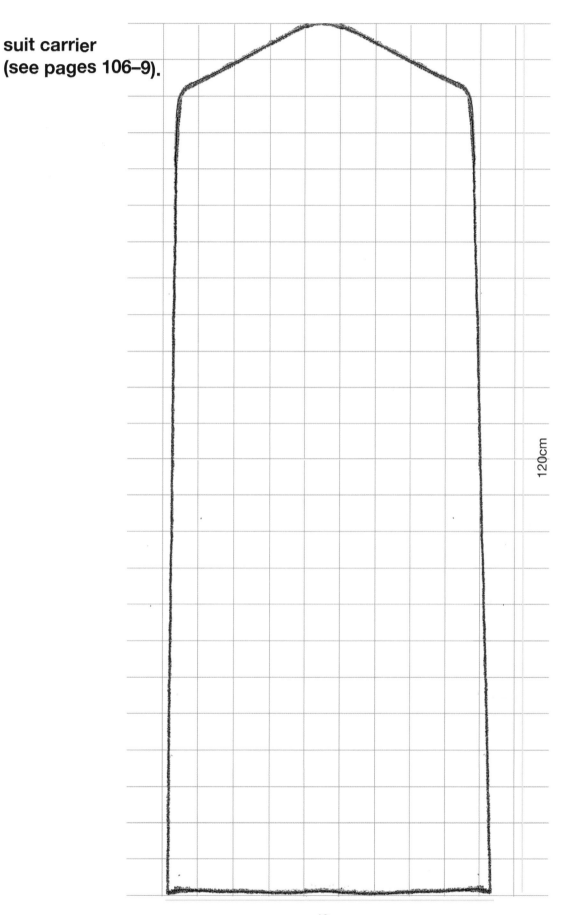

120cm

43cm

hot-water bottle cover (see pages 96–9).

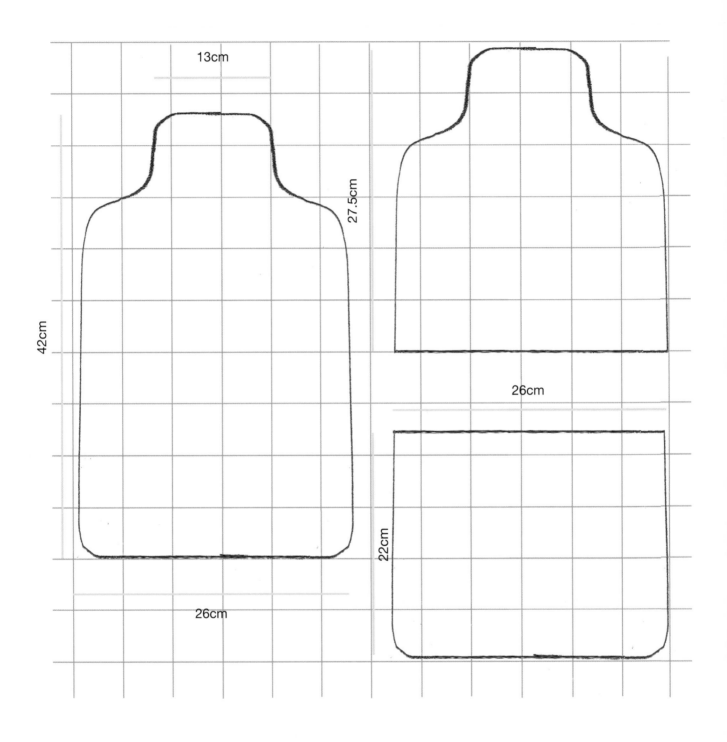

13cm

27.5cm

42cm

26cm

26cm

22cm

shops and suppliers.

beyond fabrics
www.beyond-fabrics.com
tel. 020 7729 5449.
67 columbia road, london e2 7rg.
great place to scour for fabric goodies. plus they run sewing workshops if you need any one-to-one tuition.

bell house fabrics
www.bellhousefabrics.co.uk
tel. 01580 712555.
high street, cranbrook, kent tn17 3dn.
a good range of coloured cottons, chenilles, striped and printed cottons.

john lewis
www.johnlewis.com
tel. 020 7629 771.
oxford street, london w1a 1ex.
lovely fabrics, haberdashery goods and a wide range of sewing machines.

kleins
www.kleins.co.uk
5 noel street, london w1f 8gd.
haberdashery specialist.

macculloch & wallis
www.macculloch-wallis.co.uk
tel. 020 7629 0311.
25–26 dering street, london w1s 1at.
for trimmings, threads, excellent range of fabrics and equipment.

merrick & day
www.merrick-day.com
tel. 01652 648814.
good selection of fabrics, linings, cushion pads of all shapes and sizes, plus curtain sundries, including header tape.

morplan
www.morplan.com
tel. 020 7636 1887.
56 great titchfield street, london w1w 7df.
sellers of wire coat hangers (but usually sold in bulk quantities).

nova trimmings
www.novatrimmingsltd.co.uk
tel. 01162 531144.
15 abbey gate, leicester le4 0aa.
for zips, trimmings and curtain making accessories.

russell and chapple
www.russellandchapple.co.uk
tel. 020 7836 7521.
68 drury lane, london wc2b 5sp.
great for neutral linens and denims.

sew essential
www.sewessential.co.uk
tel. 01922 722276.
a great selection of trims, threads, bias binding and lots more are available here.

the button queen
www.thebuttonqueen.co.uk
tel. 020 7935 1505.
76 marylebone lane, london w1u 2pr.
you guessed it... they sell buttons!

the clever baggers
www.thecleverbaggers.co.uk
a good stockist of quality fabric crayons.

the cloth house
www.theclothhouse.com
tel. 020 7437 5155.
47 berwick street, london w1f 8sj.
a variety of lovely cotton fabrics, linens and silks.

the cloth shop
www.theclothshop.net
tel. 020 8968 6001
290 portobello road, london w10 5te.
natural furnishing fabrics in plain, stripe and check. also great for antique blankets.

the natural curtain company
www.naturalcurtaincompany.co.uk
brilliant for cottons, linens, silks, striped and printed fabrics.

charity shops and bric-a-brac stores
these shops up and down the country great places for rummaging for lovely vintage fabrics.

acknowledgements.

many, many thanks to the following people whose generous support, encouragement and input over the past few months have helped to make this book possible.

to jane, lisa and claire for their support and expertise. to katie, the super stylist and superior spell checker, for her total understanding of my vision and wondrous encouragement. to ben for the fantastic photography and portrait patience. to mum, dad and anna for their unconditional support, love and belief in me, which goes far beyond this book. also to mum for her extensive roadtesting, instruction checking and telephone encyclopedia-type advice. to sally and glyn for the piles of 1960s sewing patterns, inspirational books and much encouragement. to jo for her support, belief, drive and sheer determination everyday. martha, emma, kangan, debbie and victor for wide-ranging brainstorming, encouragement, roadtesting, cups of tea, and general marvelousness. and to rich, everyday for his unconditional support, encouragement and love, my rock.

lisa stickley london
74 landor road
london sw9 9ph
tel 020 7737 8067
www.lisastickleylondon.com